The 2020
Poetry Marathon
Anthology

Edited by Shloka Shankar

INTRODUCTION

> A writer is a person for whom writing is more difficult
> than it is for other people. — Thomas Mann

The year 2020 saw us enter a new decade that has so far been tumultuous and rife with change. It has been an emotional, mental, political, and social rollercoaster for people all over the world.

Amidst such uncertain and turbulent times, poets from across the globe came together on June 27, 2020, to make art, embrace the spirit of camaraderie, and cheer each other to reach the finish line of The Poetry Marathon. The result of that unforgettable and memorable experience is now in your hands in the form of this exquisite anthology of poems by 192 contemporary poets.

I was given the daunting yet rewarding job of editing the anthology for this year. In her poem *Summer Morn*, Sandy Novotny notes, "...Inspiration comes in sundrops, / then in reflected rivers." As I went about reviewing submissions from so many diverse voices—expressing vulnerability, anger, loss, grief, hope, solitude, isolation, gratitude, and a multitude of other human emotions—it made me realize the healing power of art all over again. The poets in this stunning collection deserve our appreciation for not only successfully completing the marathon but also for sharing their perspectives on a wide variety of topics with such aplomb, grit, and honesty.

The anthology has been divided into two sections: Half Marathon and Full Marathon. Within each main division, I have sorted the poems loosely into themes such as nature, family, love, selfhood, protest poems, the current pandemic, and metapoems, among others. Each section's title stems from one of the poems within that section which I felt best encapsulates the chosen theme. I have always strongly believed in the collective unconscious and it can once again be seen at work in this anthology. To paraphrase the concluding line of Britton Gildersleeve's *Piecemeal*, the poets featured in this book have sung their "own pieces" to life.

I was fortunate to interact and work with so many incredibly talented poets. This project will always remain close to my heart and I'm truly grateful to the organizers, Jacob and Caitlin, for having entrusted me with this gargantuan task.

I sincerely hope you savour the contents within as you brace yourself to traverse a landscape peppered with poetic ingenuity at its best.

— Shloka Shankar

Full Marathon Poems _____12

Half Marathon Poems _____124

Index of Authors _____242

Full Marathon Poems

The Gift of Ideas

Sandy Novotny
Fayetteville, AR, USA
Hour 6

Summer Morn

The tightly-woven mesh of my chair presses
the exposed back of my leg, night's dew
damp against my thigh. Bumblebee samples
uncut dandelions as the dog sniffs it
down the line. Coffee aroma soothes me
before the vanilla-creamed sweetness
touches my tongue.

Warm burst.

All my attention focuses on loose
hair strands waltzing.

Be in the moment. Experience. Know.

See the crescent not yet to bed overhead,
out of place in risen light. The notebook
is patience in my lap, waiting for the aligning
of self. Inspiration comes in sundrops,
then in reflected rivers.

Wake up to the summer morn.

Sunanda Shome
Nottingham, UK
Hour 24

The Gift of Ideas

He gave me a present:
not store bought,
not pretty, not gift wrapped in silvery paper,
and not shoved in a box with a card on top.
He gave me an idea.

A gift wrapped in words
only thought of, not thought through,
to make my own.

"Take my gift and make it something special," he said.
"Take that idea and turn it into something magical.
Then wrap it in words and re-gift it, I won't mind.
Spread the ideas and watch as they blossom," he said.

A gift can be more than a material object.

It can be creativity that changes the world
one idea at a time.

J R Turek
East Meadow, NY, USA
Hour 21

Forgive Me, Muse

Bless me, Muse
for I have sinned.

I intentionally
misplaced 4 commas
7 times,
stole an entire line
from Shakespeare
(like he'd know),
resorted to using
2 adverbs
and 3 clichés,
rewrote Frost's
most famous poem
(I like mine better).

I defied Webster
80 times last week,
and I lied
in every poem
I've written
this year,
and last year,
and all the years
before.
I confess
I regret
none of it.

Still,
forgive me, Muse.

Deborah L. Dalton
Charlotte, NC, USA
Hour 2

I'm Rusty

My craft
it's strength
sits numb
bombarded with heavy
moments
unexamined
ungathered
ill-proper
ill-formed
paralyzed in a sea of
woe is me
amidst
global zeitgeist upheaval
craving a positive
acidic interruption
salting the foul brine
of my own
soaking
lifting
extracting
flaking away corrosive
minutia exploding into
monuments of wallowing nothingness
now dried and dusted
ready to be primed and painted
oiled with inspiration
open to a renewed
life

Cinthia Albers-Wilson
Wailuku, HI, USA
Hour 22

Hour 22

Where intelligence goes to die,
words don't make sense.
What are words?
A poem? You want a poem?
You don't want anything coherent, I'm sure.
I am here, I am typing.
I am drifting in and out of consciousness.
I cannot spell, I cannot think,
I cannot conceive of why I agree to this
year after year after year.
I am older,
weaker,
I have chemo brain.
But I keep typing
one word after another.
A sentence is our friend,
a stanza is our goal.
Beat it with brilliance:
disjointed
disillusioned
discombobulated
discombooberated.
I am sleep deprived,
word weary,
I speak gibberish now.
Perfect time to write a poem.

18

Shirley Durr
Minneapolis, MN
Hour 20

Beginning of a story I will one day write

Sheets of night rain slap steadily
against the windows,
obscuring my father's vision,
making a cozy cave for my sister and me
in the back seat.

The headlights of our Buick
illuminate the rain
barely shedding light on the lines
that carry us to journey's end.

The occasional car
passing in the lane going north
gives off sporadic blurs of brightness,
keeping steady rhythm with the miles,
keeping us in the dark.

We didn't have to ask to know
we should have been there by now.

Sandra Duncan
Portland, Victoria, Australia
Hour 8

Glyphs

I have become a translation,
a lost language spoken in
the vast space between this new
version of myself and the past.
Stalking the corridors of education,
fierce and curvaceous, almost sexy,
line upon line, I dress the future
that grows from my hands.

John Dutton
Woodbridge, VA, USA
Hour 13

Writers' Workshop

William Wordsworth wandered lonely as a cloud,
as Dylan Thomas beseeched him, "Do not go gentle into that good night."
Langston Hughes pondered to no one in particular,
"What happens to a dream deferred?"
In a heated debate all their own, J. Alfred Prufrock asked T.S. Eliot,
"Do I dare disturb the universe?"
Maya Angelou interrupted and proclaimed, "I know why the caged bird sings."
Herman Melville, for some unknown reason, wanted us to call him Ishmael,
while George Orwell swore the clocks were striking thirteen.
Charles Dickens was beside himself for he couldn't make up his mind
and kept muttering, "It was the best of times; it was the worst of times."
Sensing that the fate of the world rested on his shoulders,
Ray Bradbury struck a match and lit the collection of old parchment
he had gathered. As he watched the flames rise, he announced,
"It was a pleasure to burn the books."
This didn't sit well with Jack London for he believed
that only he knew how to build a fire.
I stood with Rebecca, and the ashes blew towards us
with the salt wind from the sea.
Robert Frost, having had enough of all of us,
called it an early night and took the road not taken home.

Amanda Potter
Jacksonville, FL, USA
Hour 12

What in the Dickinson

Awakened, ye muses,
at hour nine,
creativity spell
burned divine.

Music! Sing!
Moon shadow
strain or is it
a refrain?

Halfway there,
no need to fear.

We will make it
through the night,
my dear.

Laurie McKay
Michigan, USA
Hour 1

Mind the Children

(for Plath)

I do not know her.
Not in the sense that
does anyone really know another person,
but in the sense that
  "she lived a tormented life"
  "she was a genius"
  "she eviscerated her soul, and turned it into poetry"
  "she was narcissistic"
  "she was severely depressed"
  "she love to talk about how she would die"
  "she tried to kill herself before."
No, I do not know her.
My heart attempts to envelop her memory.
I know she still resonates
in a timely and timeless bond
shared by lost poets.
And myself.

Severely depressed, in the bleak and long winter,
she took her life.
We all know this.
We all have heard of
  her demons
  her struggles
  her glories
  her failings.
She wrote them for the whole world to see.

Yet, before she took her life,
she attended a dinner party.
Readied her children for sleep.
Left food in the bedroom for them.
Left the name of their doctor
and other information
she thought would be needed.

Yet, before she took her life,
before sealing the kitchen windows and door,
before turning on the gas,

before neatly placing a folded dish towel in the oven
(on which to lay her cheek),
before sticking her head in the oven
"as far as it could possibly go,"
she took care of her children

by leaving her coat and keys at her friend's house,
after she and the children went there for dinner,
not to have them come and stop her—no—
but to come the next day, to mind the children.

Siobhan Geraghty
Ottawa, Ontario, Canada
Hour 1

She Feeds the Soul: a tribute to the words of Maya Angelou

her thoughts trickle:
telling tales,
sowing solace,
building boundaries.
she collects tears,
leftover sentiments,
shares them
to nurture us.
her power is her pen—
it rises as a wind-drawn sail
or a well-used reel,
casting a bait of rhyme
to gather minds.
her phrases pulse with pride,
her prose preaching
a pleading prayer of her people.
a melody of meaning moves,
a rhythmic strain of hope
her mantra of survival.
anguished brows are eased,
souls sedated,
and spirits begin to soar
as her words fuse
effortlessly.
she rests as a mother should,
knowing she sustains generations
with her pages of prose.

Onoruoiza Mark Onuchi
Lagos, Nigeria
Hour 3

Kongi's Midas

His genial fire
reverberates with exotic warmth;
his aesthetically crafted tomes,
across literary modes,
exude the regal passion of a plutonic sage—
an exceptional wordsmith with lexical firepower.

Akinwande Oluwole Soyinka remains
Africa's iconic voyager of distinction,
a gadfly with the boundless depth of a pantheon.
His footprints echo the seamless craft of an art connoisseur,
his artistry reflects in his truckloads of global medallions.

A dexterous weaver of words,
a griot with uncanny wisdom of the ancients,
his priceless pearls drip with unalloyed clarity,
the striking chords of a genius.
He remains Africa's WS, a muse with matchless depth,
an inventive scholar of legendary fireworks.

Martha Custis-Miranda
Seia, Portugal
Hour 11

After Reading 'The Egyptian' by Mika Waltari

In Crete, I walked along the shoreline,
contemplating the fate of its people.
Bull gods and dancing,
a stronghold against sensibility.

I, too, could paint my breasts,
display beauty to the world.
Or focus my attention on the delicate
folds of fabric in my skirt.

In Crete, I walked along the shoreline.
Only, I was never really there.

I Am But a Weed

Rarzack Olaegbe
Lagos, Nigeria
Hour 1

May Ellen Ezekiel

it is not every day
one gets to meet a woman like you
perhaps it was the way
the heavens blessed me to have known you
perhaps it was your charm and the things you did not do
perhaps your warmth is in what you did do
hard to lay my hands on why you left your grace
and hobnobbed with the dregs in their space
rubbing shoulders with them
you gifted them the sunshine
your gap-toothed smiles lit up their day
your voice broke forth like sunrays
like a stream, you flowed freely and emptied your contents
they bathed in you to their heart's content
they dined
they wined
they smiled
like a shy sun, you sneaked away
and took your sunshine away

Joshua Factor
Durham, NC, USA
Hour 12

Eleanor Rigby

Leave the rice on the floor where it belongs.
Dreamland is not your home, no matter how much it beckons you.
Day after day you wear a surreal mask that you keep in the folds of your existence.
Don't let anyone else see it lest you vanish off the face of the earth.
And for what? Just to come home and write a speech that will never see the light of day?
No, there's more than you can perceive in any given existentialist theory,
and, when all is said and done, your memory will jump right into that grave
as you struggle to discern what it was all for in the first place.
Eleanor Rigby: the one who swam so far just to drown in shallow waters.

Amrutha B Nair
Kottayam, India
Hour 13

Green Eyes

She sat in the shadows,
brush and palette in her hand,
mixing colors again and again
to find that perfect one—

the perfect shade of green
to paint those eyes
that stared at her
from somewhere in the dream.

No, they were not just green,
they had a tint of yellow in them,
and a tiny bit of brown and blue,
and colors that were not known to her.

All the colors mixed together
and yet were separate and distinct;
her eyes spoke of stories unheard
and epics that were forgotten.

Sometimes they were like old wood,
aged well and green-brown in color.
Sometimes light green,
as fresh as a young tender leaf.

She sat there,
mixing paints,
finding the perfect shade
to paint those eyes.

Renee A. Perkins
Washington, DC, USA
Hour 18

Or You Will Be His

He chases me.
His menace singes my back.
My legs pound hard against the brittle planks.

Run, run, fast as you can
don't ever stop, or you will be his.

Smoke permeates the air, stinging my eyes into blindness.
I stumble. Fall. Panic streaks through me.
I gulp lower, fresher air then roll my feet into a sprint.

Run, run, fast as you can
don't ever stop, or you will be his.

Vision obscured, I race without compass.
I fall again. My face crunches into blood.
Perplexity floats in with a smoldering man.
Him.

Run...run...fast...as...you...can...
don't...ever...stop...or...you...will...be...
His.

Jill Calahan
Seattle, WA, USA
Hour 4

A Letter to My Reflection

Dear lost little girl,
I want you to know something—
I see you.
And when I say I see you,
I mean I am you.
We're older now,
With laugh lines that rest
In the corners of our mouth,
And crow's feet wrinkles
That highlight the twinkle
In our eyes.
But I see you.

Sometimes, I even hear you
In a belly laugh with an old pal.
Or in a whisper that carries
The joy of a secret
That you can only share
With the best of friends.

I see you.
I know you didn't get to be
That little girl for very long.
This world turns girls into women
Before they even get a chance
To enjoy what it is to be a child.
But I see you,
And I love you.

Dear lost little girl,
Come out and play,
You don't have to hide anymore.

Danielle Wong
Pierrefonds, Quebec, Canada
Hour 9

Determined to Find Her Home

She could not look at people;   their eyes moved too much.
Her eyes refused words;   they bounced on the pages.
Her thoughts ran rampant;   her tongue couldn't keep up.
Teachers said her tongue was a sign; she would never keep up.
Each day, she walked past   a shop filled with treasures:
        bones,   skeletons,   whale jaws,
            fishing nets,   schooners,   pirate ships.
She asked the owners questions;   she asked her computer.
She stored every answer   in her mind, connecting each one
        a tooth   or bone   of a fossil.
She sat silent in school,   but school was outside hours.
She was determined.   She was not factory material.
She was not institutional.   She would prove to them all.
                    She belonged to the ocean.

Note: This poem stemmed from the quote "She was determined to prove everyone wrong," as found in *Shark Lady*, by Jess Keating.

Ana Marie
Parañaque, Philippines
Hour 14

I Am But a Weed

The land knows you, even when you are lost. — Robin Wall Kimmerer

I was but a weed tucked between the slabs,
vulnerable in my little world.

I made my way through the crack,
through the crevices that split the pavers

in a sea of sharp stones and pebbles,
trampled over by unfriendly beasts.

I was small and unnoticed,
most times ignored and unappreciated,

and though in a wrong place, I grew—
with persistence, I thrived.

I am
the flower that was,

I blossom
wild and free.

I flourish
where God has placed me,

between the slabs and the edges
where dirt and running water flow,

where at the end of each day,
I gaze up at the skies

secure in the knowledge
of God's loving arms around me.

Longing

Janis Martin
Weymouth, UK
Hour 22

Sacred Rites

The moment he'd been waiting for
The whole of his twelve years
The Revered One, the Wise One
Nurturing, teaching
Training him from a babe
Those long days, those longer nights
Repeating the words and deeds
Until he got it right
And now here he was
All alone
Waiting for the setting sun
The Grandfather in the Sky
The boy entered the dank, dark cave
Water dripping, creating puddles in wells
He sat, preparing to wait a final time
As he whispered both prayers and spells
The only other noise, the sound of his breath
Then the first rays hit the floor
Spreading like wiry fingers reaching out
And he was blinded by the brilliant light
The moment had come
The boy became a man

Angel Rosen
Pittsburgh, PA, USA
Hour 2

A Recipe for a Birthday

1. An age, reluctantly announced
2. Several friends, but not enough
3. A cake that you'll eventually throw up
4. A necklace you'll never wear
5. A laugh, in unison

Choose a room, one larger than the number of people you know.
Assort your people based upon how well you know them.
Serve them cake for about 20 minutes (at least one person will decline.)
Quietly tell them they should have left their diet at home.
Open a gift, pretend you don't already have it,
shuffle your friends and hope that the joker lands on top.
Somebody cheers!
They are aware that you survived something.
Take several photos, at least one with a smile.
Post them one day later.
Accept birthday wishes for the next five business days.
Contemplate all of the birthday cards relatives forgot
to send you twelve years ago
and where those cards went when they died.

Everybody sings
or something.

Bhasha Dwivedi
Lucknow, India
Hour 8

Alive

I am tired.
Of fighting my emotions,
of discarding, suppressing
what is a part of me.

I am tired
of you telling me
my feelings are not right.
Angry at you, at myself,
for invalidating something
so true to me, to my story.

But not anymore!
I am not the same as you,
incapable of speaking up,
of voicing out what I feel.
So listen now when I say
it loud and clear:

my emotions, my feelings,
are not for you or anybody to judge.
Good, bad, positive, negative,
they are a part of me,
my story,
and my heart.

The proof that I am...
alive.

Darren Syme Coremans
Stirling, Scotland
Hour 24

Imaginary

I have often felt I am imaginary,
that I am not a real person.
I am little more than someone's pet;
perhaps this is a flawed perspective.
Can a person change how they see themselves
or within their own life do they stay neutral?

It doesn't seem possible to stay neutral;
for my feelings are not imaginary,
they are personal, only to one person.
Easily dismissed like a pet,
making me lose my perspective
when people say words which hurt themselves.

But rarely will one hurt themselves,
choosing instead, to find themselves neutral.
This strange belief is imaginary
like a fallacy dressed as a person.
I have no love for a gifted pet
lost by any other perspective.

I climb higher, seeking a new perspective;
most will never do this for themselves,
choosing ignorance in the belief it is neutral.
But inaction is intrinsically imaginary.
An unengaged, unpredictable person
who seeks not a partner but a pet.

A companion, not an equal, but a pet
is a prisoner by any other perspective.
The kept one may not see it for themselves,
believing themselves to be neutral.
Any problems they see are imaginary
if they happen to another person.

Who does that make you, what type of person?
Are you a wild lion or a house cat? A pet?
Perhaps if you pursue a new perspective
then the masses can answer for themselves.
When I have tried and failed to stay neutral,
my own ignorance becomes imaginary.

I no longer want to be an imaginary person
nor a kept pet with no outside perspective.
Defy those who defy themselves to stay neutral.

Prachi Shah
India
Hour 21

Longing

I yearn to laugh that laugh that is
unbridled, raw, pure, innocent,
the kind that comes in waves despite
your stomach knotting in stitches.
I want to choke on giggles that
make water spurt out of your nose,
that make talking impossible,
and send you rolling on the floor.
I want the laughter that starts with just one word,
a look or a knowing glance,
the laughter that comes from oft-repeated jokes,
privy only to those close to heart.
I want laughter that is the norm in on-going conversations
—transparent, unchecked, and free from judgement—
with people who are family—blood and otherwise.
I long to laugh a real laugh
that hurts your gut but feels warm inside.
It's been so long that it has turned to memory...
and now I wonder if I even can anymore.

Mel Neet
Kansas City, MO, USA
Hour 6

Matinee, Idle

You're in a movie

You are.

And the extras, for a change,
aren't walking into you.
Everyone parts for the invisible camera
that pans along your quick gait
as you walk into the Utopian Cafe
where there's always an empty seat
by the top floor window and
"everybody knows your name."

The baristas' Pandora station
has the right mix of '70s and current soul music,
so you put away your earbuds
and enjoy someone else's soundtrack
for your day.

The smell of roasting beans
wafts up to the rafters
as you reach for the ceramic mug
of dark blend, and wonder how long
you should wait before ordering
a grilled pepper and tomato sandwich
on rosemary bread.

There's time.

It's your movie. This day was the gift
you wrote for yourself
and nobody else.

There's time,
and, for once,
it's not your enemy combatant
or fellow prisoner.

It's just there,
and you're just there,
together, and so are
Al Green and Isaac Hayes.

Long shot: Sun and blue sky overhead.

44

The land knows you, even when you are lost

Stephan Kalinowski
Tucson, AZ, USA
Hour 16

Dawn

Look into the East,
the light in the sky a feast.
The planets slowly fade,
the stars close their eyes.
The night beast recuses,
the night bloomers fade.

People often miss
the wonder of dawn,
snug in their bed,
too tired to rise.
Missing the fresh blooms of morn,
the creatures of day arise.

When people awake,
the day has already been in motion.
What else will folks miss
as they go through their day?
So caught up in life are they
and oblivious to nature.

Anne McMaster
Northern Ireland
Hour 6

be thankful to the day

(in the style of ee cummings)

be thankful to the day
this precious here
this captured moment now
a place of light and loveliness
small corner bereft of morning breeze
of slowly gathering sun
this morning as the seeker, the mixer,
the chalice-bearer,
the careful, slow taster of coffee freshly brewed
so sweet and dark and strong
this golden day
be now delightedly filled with senses
open wide to the chatter of new-morning birds
and in the endless arch of a cathedral sky
to feel this weight of bones
of known flesh
of lived-in skin
that forms me on this worn spring bench
that brings me to
this perfect morning
and this moment
now

I.B.Y
Ottawa, Ontario, Canada
Hour 22

Pensive Shores

When earth touches brimming water,
and soaring height meets the solemn deep,
there is no thought left but trifling breath.

It is as though Earth and Ocean
outlined some perfect design—
between them we are dots
drawn in the horizon's line.

Claire M. Keogh
Dublin, Ireland
Hour 14

The land knows you, even when you are lost[1]

The land knows you, even when you are lost·
As does the moon, don't you go there every night?
In your sleep state, you escape the wooded trees
and the land with the earth beneath your feet
for the stilly starlight filled moonscape.
It goes to bed without you, and at night, you sleep,

perchance dreaming of the night you may
visit the moon dancing or the lunar slumber again—
the long, lonely winters with moonbeams trembling
that you witnessed so long ago, one night in summer.

1. Taken from a quote by Robin Wall Kimmerer.

Natasha Vanover
Auburn Hills, MI, USA
Hour 14

The Transcendental Nature of Plants

Plants are one of our deepest connections to the natural world.
They are the first to teach us how to flow.
We learn patience, the miraculous gift of life renewed,
and balance when we seek solitude.
These delicate creatures are extensions of ourselves.
Too much water, like too much love, can spoil us like it can rot the roots.
Too much sun, and we must learn how to spring back before it's too late,
before we hit the point of no return
and create a cause for concern.

Plants in a person's home are more telling than any art one may own.
One can keep a messy or a clean home quite easily,
yet to grow a plant one must be beyond blessed.
It is not left up to chance or fate to care for a plant,
it shows one can balance stress.
Caring for a plant shows that one is capable of love.
Romance is heavily advertised, platonic is fine, yet agape
transcends both space and time.

Plants say more about a person than you may know.
See if you have what it takes to help them grow.
Patience, caring, and knowing when to move a plant
until it finds its perfect home is a sign of empathy.
Love shared gently, given observantly,
indicates that a person has temperance and is in tune.
Plants, not unlike our tides and moon,
are as precious as seeds
for they have so many possibilities.

Mark Lucker
Minneapolis–St. Paul, MN, USA
Hour 14

Belonging

> In some Native languages, the term for plants translates to "those who take care of us." — Robin Wall Kimmerer, *Braiding Sweetgrass*

I knew from a very young age
my connection to the land—
no small feat for a city kid.

Every summer would find me
at Horseshoe Lake, nestled in
the Minnesota Northwoods.

Grandparents' retirement haven
became the same to me, once
allowed the freedom to roam.

By age nine, I knew innately
those Mission Township woods,
each sound, smell, taste, texture.

Woods have always called to me,
beckoning when I needed them,
embracing me when I arrived.

An inquisitive kid, I knew who
I could ask about anything:
Mr. Hanson knew fishing,

his wife was the bird expert,
their neighbor, Mrs. Wheeler,
was my go-to for stars, sky.

Mr. Friest understood my
spiritual nature, connections,
Mr. Holm found me amusing,

Old Man Reid knew wood,
grandma and grandpa knew a lot
about a whole bunch of things.

They all knew me and how I took

to the woods, the water, them.
They knew what the woods did.

"This kid from the big city?
Here is where he belongs.
This kid is one of us."

Beth A. Fleisher
Salem, OR, USA
Hour 22

Journey to the Light

I am stuck in darkness
but the light is before me.
I can see it clearly now,
warm and golden inside the basalt cave,
beckoning me to enter.

The journey has been long and arduous,
and I've grown weak from battle.
Starving for the light, I'm almost there.
But the worst rocks block my path now,
hundreds of them, piled high across the shoreline,
treacherous to walk across,
ready to twist and shift beneath my feet.

But that is the only path to the light,
so I must traverse it. As I step with
determination onto the first boulder,
the light from the basalt cave illuminates
a golden path across the rocks
that could not be seen from the sandy shore.
With each step I take and with each stone I conquer,
the light in front of me becomes brighter,
the pathway ahead clearer.

Moving more confidently now,
I find the boulders are anchored in my mind.
One final sprint across the last few rocks
and I'm standing at the entrance to the cave.
I stoop down to enter.
The light is so intense it penetrates to the bone,
melting all the frozen places in an instant
as light becomes music that fills the basalt cave.
I am alive. I am whole. I am dancing in light.
My body and my mind vibrate with the energy,
resonate with the frequency—
432 Hz., utter perfection in light and sound,
the eternal balance of all things.

Aaron Conklin
Warrensburg, MO, USA
Hour 14

Plant Food

I am of the earth.
My skin sheds dust like the stones shed dirt.
I am from the trees,
the leaves cradled me when I was little.
I am cyclical, seasonal, perennial.
The sun invites the best of me.

I stay distant, untouched, without belonging,
connected to the slow nights of the forest floor
where moonlight spills down through the understory.
I breathe the deep essence of the wild
into my being, through the alveoli, into my blood.
I seed the earth with my body.
Let the plants turn my corpse into a hidden garden.

Kushe Saggi
London, UK
Hour 14

Stars

Mere torches
illuminate the iconic
obsidian curtain of the night sky.
A sight to behold.
Guiding us to safety,
protecting our rest,
I haven't seen much of them lately.

Leading us toward daylight,
both toward and away from fantasy,
they glisten in multitudes
and never relinquish their hospitality.
Enveloped sometimes,
open at others
or diversifying by the second,

what matters is
at the end of the day,
they guide us past
our biggest battles.

Katelyn Dunne
Chicago, IL, USA
Hour 1

Capricornus

Once

the

rain

pours

all   you

have

left

is

a

rainbow

Meredith McGuire
Orlando, FL, USA
Hour 22

Pixie Bath

Beyond the farthest meadow,
In the center of a hill,
There rests a quiet burrow
Beneath an ice flow, never still

And in that ice-cold grotto
One can find—from time-to-time—
A tiny pixie winnow
While she bathes with wild thyme

She sings a song of summer
And she sings a song of wheat
And the melody becomes her
As she sings with voice so sweet

'Hallu, kallay, newcomer,'
She greets with words her own
'I'm seeking out a drummer
Who can sing in baritone!'

Her voice trills into laughter
Filled with honey-sweet appeal
When she finds your eyes lech after
Her shape (perfectly surreal)

'Or, perhaps you'd be a crafter
Who might make a ring f'r me?
And, if it's me y'ur heart's sought after,
You'd best know how to shrink y'ur key!'

You blink. You balk. You blunder.
Your eyes refuse to relocate,
Starry-eyed lust and in wonder
As your heart picks up its rate

And your mouth, dry as old tinder,
Hangs agape while still you stare
And you wish she'd just rescind her
Never-waning, smirking dare

But, she doesn't!

And that trill, that laugh
Carries you so high aloft,
She, you'd make your better half,
But still—speechless—you scoff!

For you cannot play a drum
And you cannot make a ring
But you know a melody! You hum,
Your deep voice lifts up to sing—

'Tis the pixie, now, who's speechless
As your voice bellows its rhyme
With a depth that leaves her breathless,
Pale-pink lips agape, this time!

Rosy cheeks deepen in color
As your song continues on
And her wings begin to flutter,
Carry her across the lawn

And she sets her lips upon yours!
Blessed kiss quells music fine;
You falter, stumble in these fervors,
Find yourself and her entwined…

…Hours later, breathless, rapturous
(Wonders never seem to cease!),
Her eyes flutter—sweet, amorous—
She sighs to you in great release:

'I teased harshly, Master Bard;
It matters not what size y'r key—
When swell of voice like that is paired
With all the singing held in me,

I can make of you a king
Or I could make of you a toad;
But I'd like from you a ring—
There's a nice shop jus' down th' road!'

Sandy Lender
Central Florida, USA
Hour 16

The Wise Green-cheeked Conure (Pyrrhura molinae)

inquisitive eyes
iridescent jade feathers
wisdom in soft purrs

Joy Miller
Escondido, CA, USA
Hour 23

A Red Racer Visit

I thought I might
drop in for a bite.

A frog or two have you here,
my dear?

SSSSurely, ssssomething to eat
amid these rocks and boxessss!

I taste it in the air, but where?
May I play with your hair?

Let's just slither over there
for a nap on these bags,

or perhaps on these rags.
What's this? A bottle of Bragg's?

I'll resssst for a while
atop your junk pile,

then slip away
to play.

Angela Mountain
Ambler, PA, USA
Hour 9

Goldilocks Regrets

"Oh, sure," drawls the woman,
her frizzy, dishwater blond hair
falling into her eyes.
"Sure, I have regrets. Doesn't everyone?"

I urge her to open up.
Share her story.
I've been steering the conversation this way
for hours.
I know who she is.
I've known since she walked into the bar,
since before she emptied the first bottle of Budweiser,
before she steadily ploughed
through a half-dozen more.

It was strange,
seeing her here.
All these years, and she's never been back.
Not that I know of, anyway.
The urgent need to hear her say it makes my heart race.
I need her confession.
I turn up the heat.

"Everyone does," I agree. Reassuring her.
Playing her.
"Mistakes happen. Kids do dumb things.
I once, accidentally, of course,
showed my dad's social security card
on a Zoom meeting.
Really stupid."

She stares into the nearly-empty bottle,
her hands curled around it, resting
on the counter in front of her.
"Yeah," she finally answers. "Kids.
Stupid, stupid kids."
She keeps staring, but finally,
the mask drops away.
The real her.

She's scared.
She's going to tell me.

"There's a cottage," she sighs.
"Not much more than a hut, really.
Just over that hill, just beyond the treeline."
A pause.
Would she tell me?
I'm so close now.
So close.

"I hate porridge, you know?"
The non sequitur hurtles toward me.
She's had a lot to drink.
"I hate porridge so damn much."
My heart races.
Here it comes.
The moment of reckoning. Except,
it's not.

She sighs.
"The porridge in the cottage. It was actually good."
She gazes blankly at that blasted bottle.
"So good. I've hated porridge ever since.
It's not fair, you know?"

And then she looks at me,
slowly smiles.

Not a nice smile. A sly smile.
"Know what else I hate?" she smirks.
"Bears."

And, running her cool eyes over
my warm brown fur,
my massive paws,
my quivering snout,
she says it again.
For emphasis.
"I hate bears."

Heart Gallery

JL Nash
Yorkeys Knob, Australia
Hour 18

Tick-tock Holiday Clock

Tick-tock, the clock is dead.
No one checks what the kids watch
on TV when they are on their own.
Rrrring the phone is broken.
It doesn't take time to stare
out into space, so you can do it
as much as you like;
you will never be late.

It's the usual story:
parents fighting,
gas lighting each other.
It's so common, it would feel strange
if there wasn't a row first thing in the morning.
And, of course, the beginning of the disappearing
Umhlanga Rocks.[1] Or was it Sands?
It no longer matters,
it was catastrophic, regardless.

"You'll love Christmas on the beach,"
they promised, and we as kids
agreed with whatever was presented
upon the table. Traditions and promises
weren't kept in our family.
Survival was to be flexible enough
to spin on a quarter and keep smiling
far longer than you oughta.

Tick-tock, the clock is dead.
No one checks on who talks
to the kids at the beach.
Rrrring the phone is broken.
It doesn't take a shrink to analyse
they're telling us lies again.

Presents opened on a hotel floor
lack the panache and grandeur
of discoveries at home.
Amongst the ordinary,
even parcels brightly wrapped

and as large as a fingernail
would be pronounced magic.

There's no room to play
so the toys are packed away.
It's down to the beach for a holiday
of watching long walks and disappearances;
the kids play in the surf
and watch the adults play tag.

Tick-tock, the clock is dead.
No one checks on who gives out
memories to the kids to keep.
Rrrring the phone is broken.
They had to be so much more inventive
before we became attached to technology.

1. Pronounced as *um-sh-l-anga.*

Daria Lebedeva
Sweden, Älmhult
Hour 4

Iron Mum

Her mother, at her best, had only one daily care:
"feed up ungrateful pups, no smile however rare."
Severe, stone-hearted, ever busy with the household,
her mother was that kind of woman who was ignored and bold;
in rare moments she came to mum with a toy,
half-broken, with a blurred stamp of a past child's joy,
a plea in her voice: "Could you play with me?"
"Wait a moment!" A promise never to be...

Ramona L. Elke
Maple Ridge, BC, Canada
Hour 23

Arthur

I don't remember
when he first came
to talk to me in mirrors,
or when we would play cards.
Or, at dinner time,
when I would beg my mother
to set him a place at the table
so he could eat with us;
he was always hungry
and lonely.

I would call him
on my red play phone
and we would talk
for hours and hours
about his day,
and all the great adventures
he would get up to.

Forty years later,
I met him again
in a Great War Cemetery in France
(Sunken Road Cemetery),
buried near a lad
with my daughter's middle name.
I know he was "real."
Arthur was my relative...
never really imaginary,
he was just never visible
to anyone but me.

Gemma Hinton
Selsey, West Sussex, UK
Hour 12

Not Personnel

The seats faced backwards
so medical personnel could face the patients...

I was not personnel;

I was a 6-year-old child flying home with my mother
on the only flight available
to get 'home' from home—RAF Wildenrath—quickly.
So we sat there obediently,
my phobias and I,
wincing each time the curtains were drawn back to reveal
one of the nurses administering some treatment that was necessary
or providing pain relief—at least to some degree.
My hands were clasped in a prayer, hoping it would
not involve blood.

I was not personnel;

I was a 6-year-old girl
with—what at the time I had no way of being able to tell—
what was only *later* understood,
a Most Peculiar Childhood.

Vivian Rose
Oceanside, NY, USA
Hour 16

Sisterhood

Blanketed in protection from the outside world,
I work to shield her, she works to shield me.
I hold her hand, her warmth, and admiration,
something I crave more than the sun, more than air,
because she is my sister;
and in the end, she's the only one that really matters.
She and I, seemingly born on opposite ends of the world,
find ourselves making our way closer and closer
to each other every day as we age.
She learns from me, the many mistakes I've made,
so her pain won't be the same as mine ever was.
I adore her, comfort her, know her, and call her
when my knees start bleeding from the harshness of this world,
when my tears become too bitter,
when society seems so cold and lonely.
Her smile hugs me tight, her eyes tell all of her secrets,
her voice as sharp as a critic, her legs as fast as the wind.
She's my best friend,
like a favorite pen, a good read, a refreshing swim on a hot day.
I need her and she needs me;
that's simply how it is.

Ashley "LuvMiFreely" Powers
Dayton, OH, USA
Hour 22

Heart Gallery

Welcome to my heart gallery!
Let me take you on a tour.
It all began inside my mother's womb,
perfectly designed by the Father,
beating to give me life.
Once I made my exit into this world,
my mother could no longer protect it.
Here, to your right, is the first sign of damage:
it's a little bruised but nowhere close to shattered.
The description reads,
"The day her dad abandoned her."
Now, to your left, you will notice the damage is a little more intense.
Description reads,
"Abuse from someone who was supposed to love her."
Down the hall, the damage has turned to small cracks from it being mishandled.
If you look closely, it reads,
"Suicide is never the answer."
Across from this one, the damage is extremely noticeable.
The description states,
"Gave to the wrong person. He used her and turned her into a single mother."
Behind this glass, this one is shattered but still in one piece.
It reads,
"Losing loved ones can leave you hollow. Fragile, hold with caution."
As you can see in this glass case,
this one has been completely broken.
The description states,
"This is what happens when you lose your mother."
In this room you'll see it's been put back together;
cracks are still visible, held together with superglue.
This plaque quotes,
"I can do all things through Christ who strengthens me. Phil 4:13"
Let me end this tour with a reminder:
Life won't always give you kindness.
Some people will love you
and some will come to kill, steal, and destroy you,
but God has the final say in your ending.
You can either let circumstances break you
or you can use those trials and be an inspiration.
Give it all to God and let Him heal you.
As long as He gives you breath,
you have the chance to start over.
Thank you for coming!

Mandi Smith
Balch Springs, TX, USA
Hour 4

Forever Bound

Grief
is like
a rusty chain
wrapped tightly 'round
a tree
trunk,
slowly
sinking deeper
into the wood,
weighing heavy on
our hearts,
suffocating,
stealing
light from
our eyes, breath
from our bodies,
leaving us
empty,
until
one morning
we awake, only
to discover we
can breathe
again,
for
the chain
has grown to
become a permanent
part of
us.

Ojo Blessing
FCT, Abuja, Nigeria
Hour 18

Perhaps Father Should Have Taught Me Songs Heal

Grief and solitude are brothers of destruction—
my dictionary says they can be used interchangeably.
My father was teaching me to be a hard man,
how not to smile. He believed smiles make one too soft,
like wet earth for sorrows to creep in, burrowing holes
for more woes to find ranches. In one of his lessons,
he said I needed to learn to bottle grief in my body,
that men don't cry. This means killing the tear glands in my eyes.
But the day the news of mother's journey beyond
reached him, he broke into constellations of dirges.
He screamed as if mother once lived in his voice,
and singing aloud would resurrect her. I realized then
that he was seeking healing in the arms of a requiem.

Vijaya Gowrisankar
Mumbai, India
Hour 3

Grateful for Is

A few minutes ago, our relationship was an *is*.
Soon after, my world tilted and our relationship
became a *was* as one heart breathed its last.
From conversations and laughter,
the equation changed to memories
that evoked pain, denial, numbness, and shock.

I ran, I ran as fast as my legs could take me...in my mind

Yet, I was rooted to reality. I couldn't run away
from the phone calls that had to be made
and all the arrangements for the last rites.
People gathered, some, taking over.
Familiar faces...yet, a blur...neighbors, friends, relatives.
Thirteen days passed. The pillow still held his scent,
I could still hear his voice resonate within the walls.
I could feel him hug me in my dreams, only to awaken to harsh reality.

I ran, I ran as fast as my legs could take me...in my mind

"Will today's sunrise be any different?" I asked myself each day for a year.
Things changed as time passed...I forced myself to start healing.
My family looked at me with hopeful eyes, prodding me to embrace life.
That's what my father would have wanted for us all.
Loss taught me a lesson: to value those who are with me today,
at this moment, and appreciate them before *is* becomes *was*.

I ran, I ran as fast as my legs could take me...in my mind

Amy Laird
Spencer, IA, USA
Hour 14

For My Father

Hey Daddy,

It's me again. I know it's
tedious hearing from me
over and over again;
I just can't seem to stop
reaching out to you.

I was thinking about
you today—
I received a wheat penny
at the store today and I
almost broke down.

I didn't though,
and I know I'm going to be
alright. That I'm not ready
to see you again just yet.

That's OK though—as much as
I miss you—
there's so much I am doing
these days.

I'm making friends,
I have a job I really like,
I have family around me,
I am living on my own
in my own place
and I like it.

I don't have much time right now
to tell you everything that has
been going on because there is
just so much and so many things
going on with me, I can't seem
to narrow it down.

But I'm OK, Daddy.
I can let you go now

and I can and will survive
without you here on earth.

That's not to say I don't miss
you, Daddy, because I do, every
single day. But I'm stronger now
and I will be OK.

I love you, Daddy, so much.

Love,
Me

Tamara Dillon
Danville, IL, USA
Hour 16

I'm Her Daughter, Too

She always says, "I'm so sorry,"
no matter how many times
I tell her "It's fine."
She'll always be my mom.
Taking care of her
is my privilege,
not my duty.
She'll eventually forget me.
I know it's the
disease but my heart
will still break.
She was always independent,
a woman on the move,
always taking care
of everybody.
She's precious to me.
I'll always be there,
even when she forgets
I'm her daughter, too.

Tobe T Tomlinson
Vermont, USA
Hour 13

Storm Chaser

Endless years a single mother,
I am now maternally unemployed;
I watch *Twister* too many times,
knowing the work was similar.

Six grandchildren later,
I am the meteorologist
providing forecasts and
confirming normal patterns.

Despite overcast behaviors,
major events thus far avoided,
there is no talk of possible
thunder, lightning, flooding.

My tornadoes barely survived
my children now parents—
I can still see the pickup
lifted by the Twister.

Cynthia Hernandez
Seattle, WA, USA
Hour 5

Blanketed in Light

Light spills
into the gap
between
here and gone
yesterday and tomorrow
what is and what will be.

Walk the
illuminated path
to the other side.

When you get there,
turn and wave.

A recognition of the distance
you've traveled.

A greeting to those
walking their own paths

blanketed in light.

Margarette Wahl
Long Island, NY, USA
Hour 4

Legacy

Give me a metaphor for the moment. — Harriet Slaughter

Remember me in metaphors, not in everyday clichés.
Remember my written words,
how I spilt my heart across the page.
Remember me for my good deeds,
the ways I intended the world to be.
Remember me inside the scents of roses and of daisies.
Remember me in the touch of rain on your cheeks,
inside the sincerity of ballads on the radio.
Remember me in the sweetest taste of raspberries.
Remember me like a song, one you repeat over and over,
never growing tired of its entirety.
My legacy will continue as you move on.
I'll be the bittersweet side of your history.

Megan R. Saturley
Orlando, FL, USA
Hour 18

A Christmas Casserole

It's not the main course, so it's not a huge deal,
but wouldn't it be a drag to be eaten by our meal?
The tuna casserole did not turn out according to plan,
and I just heard growling coming from the metal pan.

"I think you made it mad," whispered my husband.
"Did you add something weird? Strychnine or red onion?"
"Keep your voice down," I whisper in a panic.
If we aren't careful this concoction could turn volcanic.

Was it the mushrooms? Or the sour cream?
Making this dish was my only holiday dream!
Bringing to life a tradition from our family's past,
but this is not the type of conjuring I meant to forecast.

Even topped with breadcrumbs it's not the least bit attractive.
It almost looks like it's glowing, possibly even radioactive.
I wish I was being even the least bit satirical,
but to make it out of the kitchen alive we'll need a real Christmas miracle.

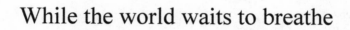

While the world waits to breathe

Anda Marcu
Ontario, Canada
Hour 1

Cattail

You could see right through me,
you said to me once, and I laughed
because I found myself tongue-tied
but didn't want silence to take over.
I had to chase her away
with rolling specks of sonance.

Stained fingers from picking berries
and eating them one by one;
swallow them whole,
distracted.
Probably thinking of a lake
bordered by tall cattail.

Jessica Gershon
Ripley, TN, USA
Hour 3

Viridiphile

I can only imagine a winter day
naked of verdure.
Plants rooted in earth's clay,
flowing with contour,
verdant eyes gazing
the day I was born—
a love so amazing,
it stings like a thorn;
a color between blue and yellow
where the sun kisses the skies,
I run through green meadows
every time I look into your eyes.

Nicole Harlow
Canoga Park, CA
Hour 16

Untitled

dizzying
  my thoughts center on you
every waking moment
 I catch my breath
stealing glances at time
  the day goes by
then
  I see you through the doors
skipping a beat
 your smile wraps around my heart
sets my soul on fire

Ivan Bekaren
Lagos, Nigeria
Hour 10

Baby Midnight Train

the soliloquy of the midnight train
reminds me of a future past,
a future past
where your smile is the sun
that seeps past the windowpane
to light up this room
where i stare, as you do,
into a fine presence that warms
this space with bliss;

the train passes
and i hear your giggle
as i close my eyes to sleep;
in the home of my lover's arms,
recalling future pasts
from a dream tavern
forged from the finest gold,
overlooking a lively city
that refuses to sleep,

your voice sends me to sleep,
it sends me to sleep

dextajean
Russellville, AR, USA
Hour 6

While the world waits to breathe

While the world waits to breathe again,
      I inhale the scent of you.
      My nostril hairs tingle, and the back of my throat purrs
      before I can stop it.
      My body searches for your rhythm,
      and my every movement matches yours.
      My body rises and falls with the breath from your lungs,
      and we dance to a silent song.
      While the world waits to breathe again,
      together we exhale.

Tracy Plath
Franklin, IN, USA
Hour 6

Dichotomy

I awaken to electrically charged air particles
standing the hairs of my arms up at attention,
the bed a warm cocoon holding at bay
a world awash in rain.

The crackling energy is both felt and heard
in thunderous crashes and booms,
reverberating through sternum and heart.

I step out beneath the overhanging roof past the door,
daring to enter the domain between my safe interior
and a world no longer my own with warmth at my back
and wildness in my face.

The storm subsides to a murmur as I step further out,
the soaked hem of my long dress slapping my ankles
as I bury my face in the humid, red scent
of newly opened roses, droplets trickling down face and arms.

I turn, a renewed wild creature,
and turn and turn again,
falling to the wetness beneath my feet,
breathing the earth through my skin.

Finally I am chilled and soaked, abashed, and ready to return
to my civilized home, stripping bare and sharing the warmth beneath
feathered down comforters with my waiting love.
Through delicate touches and wondering kisses, I blend
the wild without and the warm within.

Brandee Charters
Dayton, OH, USA
Hour 20

Misty Whispers

i kiss you tonight
from so very far away
and yet i feel
closer to you than ever before

i close my eyes
and open my self
for your tender caresses
the whispers of my name
on your silken lips

the way you feel
so hard against me
fingers in my hair
love all over my face
eyes inside my soul

as you hold me
turning me with your passion
under streetlights
in the rain for hours
never noticing strangers

driving past
staring
jealously

Carol Titus
Indianapolis, IN, USA
Hour 12

Music & Wine

words, secrets, hopes, dreams,
a warm hug,
a quick kiss,
whispered words,
a soft caress,
comfortable silence
yet electricity in the air

tilted glasses,
nectar of the vine,
deep conversations,
feelings heavy & astute
blur the edges,
thoughts tumbling in my
cloudy brain

Lindsey Toya-Tosa
Jemez Pueblo, New Mexico, USA
Hour 19

love vs. love

i realize i never tell you i love you.
it's not because i don't, i do,
you just no longer deserve to hear it.
my "i love you" would hit you
like a confetti bomb,
the sudden boom of my words and the confetti
sticking to you for eternity.
my love stays with you
until you are sick of it.
you tell me you love me multiple times a day.
throwing the words around like unclaimed packages,
you hope someone will claim them
but they end up getting thrown away or forgotten.
your love doesn't stay,
it strays.
your "i love you" is used when you no longer know what to say,
filling the conversation void.
it saves our relationship from getting "awkward."
my "i love you" is not to be taken lightly,
because, even once we're through,
i'll still love you...

Crystal T. Davis
Portland, OR, USA
Hour 4

Exoneration

Dear Curtis,
the scars you left
belong to me now;
thank you for the gift.

Del Bates
Shelby Township, MI, USA
Hour 1

Heart on Hold

broken heart,
tears now fall.
I do not under
stand at all.

why this pain
of being alone?
no more joy
within my home.

I'm so alone,
where are you?
what am I
supposed to do?

yes, heaven has
called your name.
how can I
ever be the same?

but when my name
is called, we'll be
re-joined as one
for eternity.

The World's an Ashtray

Bia Riaz
Tomball, TX, USA
Hour 14

Plant kingdom

It started with a fire
Blazing hot brutal devastating
howling winds with forked tongues
licked flames
kicking them higher
melting metal shattering glass
obliterating concrete
human screams lost in raging infernos
crawling across the planet
all was charred all was scarred
a wasteland

Time passed

It started with the seeds
tiny sprouts pushing through
deep dark well rested soil
stronger than before

spreading leaves extending branches
smiling at the sun
showering in the cooling rains
birds chirping bees buzzing
visiting newly blossomed flowers
sucking nectar spreading pollen

Mother Nature hummed and mused
It was time to bring them back
the flora and the fauna
all except the humans
there was no longer any place for them
in Paradise

Ian Barkley
Champaign, IL, USA
Hour 3

Something Real

The devil went down to Louisiana
looking to find a decent meal,
surrounded by beggars, as he often is,
all imploring him to make a deal.
He rubbed his knee and lamented his fate:
"I hate my job but it makes good money,

dressing wounds that will never heal."

He picked one out, "God's favorite, I guess,
we're at the crossroad, state your appeal."
"I've searched for money, God, and sex,"
Man said, "something, anything, to make me feel.
But still I stand here, empty, numb,
spinning round and round that dharma wheel.
Give me something to believe in, something true,
something eternal I know is real. I'm sick of

hiding wounds that will never heal."

The devil flipped through his contracts, checked his commission,
said, "Prick your finger, sign here in blood, your fate is sealed."
Man stumbled away in pain, leaving a trail he couldn't conceal
as his finger dripped, dripped blood forever.
The devil walked on limping, still hungry, without a meal.
He makes good money but can never find the time for he's

too busy making wounds that will never heal.

Sandra Johnson
Houston, TX, USA
Hour 22

The World's an Ashtray

The world's a giant, sooty ashtray;
holes in walls, smoke-black stains
our sins, the earth's full burning pain
the trash we dump in bucket loads—
glass on sidewalks, crushed in roads,
they cut the ground with fractured nodes.

Each hole spies a different window
where shadows lurk and poisons go;
a ghost of once a rugged life
got tired and offed his scathing wife
then stabbed himself with a knife.

Graffiti it will sometimes be,
the smoking offal of gangs and rings.
Drugs, they rot people about,
smacking loves and lives near inside-out.

Drunks wreck homes and highways
then steal others' days.
Pollution is the slow demise
of our land and skies.
Developers, ever-promising trees
I know that I will never see,
land finally will a desert be.

Burning, screaming volcanoes
will torch what's left in fiery throes;
when the ashes cool and finally mend,
creation can begin again.

William Aswell
Los Angeles, CA, USA
Hour 7

Anxiety

Flowing time, internal grinding mechanical compulsion,
incessant on-going harsh driving onwards,
sound grabbing all space from subtler resounds,
engulfed by lightless darkening.
All potency drawn into this machine,
stretched out constantly tired,
willfully compelled built that one avenue,
clinging only where magnets can grab.
Weary surrender curling up like drying leaf,
low continued supplication, release the outside,
cradle torment in fetal form.
Corrosive endless weakness manhandle on itself,
mask painted brave outside,
whirring-on hoping to get out alive.

Janice Raquela Mendonca
Melbourne, Australia
Hour 21

Human Craving

I crave deep, meaningful connections.
I long for honest, unfiltered conversations
with absolutely anyone who is willing to pour their heart out.

In the age of social distancing,
I miss the human touch,
the healing power of a hug,
the warmth in a handshake—
the reassurance and confidence
that lies in a firm, confident grip.

I crave unique communications that expand beyond mere words.

While everybody is busy hoarding up,
I have learned the harsh reality of greed
and its capacity to erase humanity.

But I still crave the human touch.
I want to feel human again...

Alas! The immune system isn't immune to everything.

Elizabeth Durusau
Athens, GA, USA
Hour 22

Just a Hug

Someone in the chat said,
"I wish I could cuddle someone."
Every person living alone
on the other side of the keyboard
felt a hard jerk on their heartstrings,
trying to remember the last time
they were touched by affection.
I replied, "At this point, I'd settle for just a damn hug."

Shobha Elizabeth John
Kerala, India
Hour 23

Sunset

Today I saw the sun set
and the birds return
—the day's work done
for the twenty-sixth day in a row—
from my cobwebbed window.

I dream of home:
sunflowers in the garden,
curry on the stove,
grandmother's clock,
a blanket that smells like hope.

I wither away
within these walled minutes,
longing to leave,
to sing, to flee.
But the world outside is caught
in perpetual dusks without end
like me, a story with no resolution,
a beautiful song going on for too long.

I sigh and remember
the Little Prince, alone
as he watched his forty-four sunsets;
how often we smile when sadness
becomes too heavy to bear.

Riley Mazzocco
New York City, NY, USA
Hour 7

Season of the Sirens

The children who live by the lake
swim in it all summer long,
but they know never to go swimming
when the chill of autumn arrives.
For it is when the sirens return.

The sirens swim back to the lake,
the warm water drives them away.
Every year dozens of tourists fall prey,
which is why the sirens stay.
The haunting melody of their song
ruining lives as they go on.

Their voices never falter.
They show no mercy.

Tessa Mountain
Ambler, PA, USA
Hour 24

Gift of Life

my mom-mom has a gift waiting for me:
a Christmas cactus.
her daughter told her
about my growing plant collection,
so she took a cutting
from her own mother plant
to give to me
when next we meet.
I cannot go to get it
while the virus rages on.
one little piece of cactus
isn't worth the risk.
she has survived
past childhood (several siblings didn't)
through cancer and its toxic treatment.
I would give all my leafy children
plus some hundred more
so that this, too,
she strides past
to give her gifts herself.

Ayafa Tamuno-Tekena
Lagos, Nigeria
Hour 16

Brief

Some say legends are born, while others say they are made; I guess it all depends on your perspective.

Legends are people who have overcome difficult circumstances, not minding their status or giving excuses to serve as limitations and barriers for why they couldn't accomplish a certain goal.

It's so unfortunate that the mortuary hosts celebrations daily and they are served the unrealized dream or goal that didn't come to fruition because your breath was taken from me.

Hope is only a grain of sand, for we don't know when we will bid this world farewell.

An Ordinary Peace

David L. Wilson
Wailuku, HI, USA
Hour 1

The Problem Is That

we all are aware
a cop would never
press his blue knee
down
against the white neck
of an Ivy-Leaguer

Lynny F
Long Island, NY, USA
Hour 10

Made of Stone

Hidden away
in walls of gray
are the stories
made of stone.

Sitting in sight
and showing all their might
are the stories
made of stone.

Showing their history,
uncovering the mystery,
through the people
made of stone.

Kendra Reynolds
Northern Ireland
Hour 7

Season of the Revolution

Can you hear it?
The wind twisting her voice around a new syllable,
dropping the lyrics of a contemporary song.

Can you feel it?
The sun's oppressive anger waning,
focused now on her cool baptismal light
christening us all into the new order.

Can you see it?
Young buds surging with fresh growth,
climbing fences, cracking walls,
splashing diverse colour on this grey canvas.

Can you taste it?
The grainy depth of values distilled and consumed
giving way to the sweet ripeness of new wines;
progressive labels and ethical processes.

Can you touch it?
The hand of your partner, lover;
the hearts of your two mothers;
the dream that seemed so out of reach.

Can you smell it?
The fermenting fear of the system
unaccustomed to sharing.
For this is the season of change.

Gina Gil
Arlington, VA, USA
Hour 21

An Ordinary Peace

I long for a deep sleep
not the fairy tale kind that involves a curse or a kiss
just an ordinary bed with just the right amount of covers
allowing me to sleep in comfort without a reason to toss and turn

I long for sweet dreams
not the kind that are so involved that I feel like
I have been up all night living a double life
just an ordinary dream that feels cozy and maybe even forgettable

I long for peaceful days
not the kind that involves having to navigate crowded trails and sidewalks
with people who hang out in big groups and don't wear masks
just an ordinary day where picking up a few vegetables at the farmer's market
and some bread at the bakery isn't a strategic maneuver

I long for a calmness in the world
not the kind that involves denying the hard truths of our society
but rather a calmness from addressing the tragic structures and failures
and choosing right-action to set a new course

I long for a rest for those who have fought so hard
to ensure the rights of themselves and others

They deserve to rest and be at ease

The Ultimate Gift

Roxann Harvey-Lawrence
Jamaica
Hour 24

The Ultimate Gift

The gift that matters most in life,
the gift that holds the keys to your destiny—
is it the gift of peace, the gift of joy,
the gift of happiness, or is it the gift of love?
What truly matters is the ultimate gift;
one that holds no bars,
no favors, no grudges, no handles.
The gift that teaches, guides, protects, heals,
brings us all back to remembrance—
seek for it today. It is available to all.
The ultimate gift is what matters most in life!

Viswo Varenya Samal
Keonjhar, India
Hour 15

Plane Trip

taking off from the airport
and landing at the place of choice
is but a matter of two breaths:
in between there are clouds
where the essence of life is laid out

Dr. Vishnu Unnithan
Mumbai, India
Hour 24

All Hail My Almighty Powerful Lord

All hail my Almighty Powerful Lord.
Devout, rich, atheist, sinner, meek, and poor,
His every subject He does reward.

His benevolence always strikes a chord,
dues are paid in due course, this He makes sure.
All hail my Almighty Powerful Lord.

Through time and space, each creation and pea pod,
He showers His grace on them all once more.
His every subject He does reward.

Our every action He does record,
only to see whether our heart stays pure.
All hail my Almighty Powerful Lord.

Even our sins He erases from our board,
if we truly rue what we did before.
His every subject He does reward.

Though non-believers may swear by their sword,
any snag, He has a miraculous cure.
All hail my Almighty Powerful Lord.
His every subject He does reward.

S. Rupsha Mitra
India
Hour 22

In the City

The city embraces me
in its entirety—its twisting narrow lanes
in the aftermath of a heavy rain
like the aftertaste of an aromatic aura.
The scent of soil
intermixes with the haze
like the smoke
rising from the Dhunachi.[1]
A sudden flickering of the lantern—
satori.
The Victoria Memorial picturesque
in lucent moonlight,
the race course darkened,
expansive.
The National Library, in dark and shadow,
a chiaroscuro in lamppost lights.
My city comes alive like this
at times.

1. A Bengali incense burner used for one of the stages during aarti, or ritualized dance worship.

Joaquin Capehart
Queens, NY, USA
Hour 17

I Let My Tape Rock Till My Tape Pop

Back in the '90s
when cassette tapes were
still in style,
we practiced patience;
putting on our favorite station,
we waited on the radio
to play our top tune,
being careful not to hit
the record button too soon.
As we listened to the boom box
bump Biggie's *Juicy*
until we were hypnotized,
fire hydrants gushed
extinguishing that New York sizzle.

David Bruce Patterson
Ontario, Canada
Hour 23

Leftovers

We all stood in a wide circle,
toasting the last of the champagne.
The evening went by as quickly
as the teasing champagne.

I helped with the jackets
and offered Tupperwared portions
and any wine that was sitting
in unconquered portions.

I walked out to the driveway
with the satiated company
for the goodbye waves
as they drove away from my company.

But there was no loneliness,
just joy.
A reflection of thankfulness,
the most fulfilling kind of joy.

I knew something was forgotten
— there always is—I was aware
and saw a silk scarf
on a now lonesome chair, so unaware.

Sam Azule
Queens, NY, USA
Hour 15

Tequila Sunrise

I'm ready to go
with a natural lippie
and some eyeliner.
I'm ready to take the town,
ready to have a drink,
dance with my girls,
tear this shit down.
I'm not really one for besties
but with Cuervo & I?
It's a vibe.
I'm sandwiched between
good music, my girls,
& my favorite guy.
I want to dance
out of my heels
under the midnight sky.
A wild mama
doin wild things
& livin' wildly
with Jose
'til sunrise.

Valkyrie Kerry
Mayo, Ireland
Hour 13

Tattoo Artist

A scraping sting carves into her shin,
the spider of sin.

Magic ink brings the spider to life,
subdued with a knife.

Sweat beads form under his threat;
he drools as the spider crawls.

Climbing her rigid corpse, a tear falls.
He takes a deep breath as his creation climbs,
a death bite to the nipple, sublime.

Spider of sin, subdued with a knife, the spider crawls.

Molly Hickok
Mountain View, CA, USA
Hour 20

The Little Pyro

Click, whoosh! the flame sprang to life
Click, zwoop! the flame died again.

On and off like a switch,
not really serving a purpose,
it was mindless, focused.

And as you watched it flicker,
something stirred in the darkness.
A feeling, somewhat profound,
somewhat dangerous, but without sound.
No words described the need you felt
to make the lighter click.

Click, whoosh! the flame in your mind sprang
Click, zwoop! the flame died once again.

Deanna Ngai
Airdrie, Alberta, Canada
Hour 20

The Streetlamp

The streetlamp sheds its gentle glow
  across the street from me.
It spreads its light in the darkness,
  enabling me to see.
Rain trickles from its top,
  a misty waterfall.
It drips and falls to the ground
  like sparkles that enthral.
Thank you, streetlamp, from my heart,
  for sharing your bright light.
You help me see in the darkest of times,
  even during this never-ending night.

Half Marathon Poems

Into the Wilderness

Jenifer Faylor
Everett, WA, USA
Hour 1

Bluebirds at Dawn

The bluebirds' holy wings
carve invisible sculptures
in the morning's mossy
green air. They chirp
scriptures that raise
the sun from its tomb
(down to their last feathers
they don't believe in doom).
They flit from the real
to the electric
trees rooted in the street,
and, simple as a sunstroke
in the world's luminous tapestry,
deliver their daily love
letter, note by note,
to every creature they meet.

Anne Paterson
Calgary, Alberta, Canada
Hour 9

Dancing on Wings

Plump Geese join the band of Jays amid a colony of Gulls.
Finches charm the mob of Emus
while the parliament of Owls shares their wisdom.
Nightingales watch the deceit of Lapwings, bringing the Hawks to boil.
The congress of Crows scares the Doves into flight
while the Flamingos stand pat.
Chickens brood over paddling Ducks,
the chattering Starlings upset over the unkindness of Ravens.
Swallows gulp at the Woodpeckers' descent,
a pandemonium of Parrots scatters.

Darkness falls,
the Dance of the Wings has closed.
The party is over,
good night.

Cristy Watson
Surrey, BC, Canada
Hour 7

season of the bohemian waxwing

when i tipped my feathers with red
and floundered in the forest of yellow cedars,

stood shakily on the branches of the blackberry bush
intoxicated with fermented fruit,

thinking i had found a spruce for building
my nest and mating...

but a winter of snow
meant road salt in the spring water

that turned my insides bitter
and left me without young

for years to come

Utkarsh Sharma
Houston, TX, USA
Hour 9

Rust Belt

The hum of the cottage AC fills the evening air.
Empty bottles decorate the porch with diffracted light.
Heat pitter-patters on the mid-western breeze
as fireflies emerge for their nightly performance.

This ode to classic Americana has faded into the fringes.
With its purpose fulfilled, it lies waiting for a new suitor.

Jana O'Dell
Charleston, WV, USA
Hour 12

Into the Wilderness

Like the mountain lion who holds her own
and comes upon the cliff top looking deep down,
I feel my oneness—
a calling
within the wilderness.
Like the snake that slithers from woodsy grass
to open waters,
I feel my oneness—
a calling
within the wilderness.
Like the bird that nests atop trees,
looking down to protect the ones she loves,
I feel my oneness—
a calling
within the wilderness.
Like the mama cub who protects her young,
ready to pounce on anyone who threatens their safety,
I feel my oneness—
a calling
within the wilderness.

Anne Farmer
Buckner, MO, USA
Hour 11

Mary Oliver's Woods

I've never been to Mary Oliver's woods.
The sunlight and shadow-filled woods which wrapped her in words
that she spelled out in spilled ink
so that we might read,
and, in a sense,
arm-in-arm, eyes turned upward and onward
languidly walk with her,
and her wild, curly-haired dogs, loving and leading
the way past anxiety in a place that
reveals wonderment and a comfortable lack of fear.

Lena C Hairston
Upland, CA, USA
Hour 22

Quietness Reigns

quietness is kept
when all is spent,
if only you can see
beyond your "me"

blue and lavender hues
will lend a cue
to possibility
of serenity

above the mountains,
beyond the clouds,
in silenced refrains
quietness reigns

Nancy Canyon
Bellingham, WA, USA
Hour 5

Time Slows on Corral Hill

The sound of nothing is constant here at 6,000 feet: breezes rustle treetops, heat wafts up the draws. We feel slow. Slow muscles. Slow to speak, slow to answer. Slow to proceed. It is almost as if we sleepwalk through our days. There is hauling water, recording weather stats, preparing meals. And always, we search for fire; this evening we watch the sun go down, orange-yellow light igniting the valley. The forest seeks our eyes. We see chipmunks, ravens, eagles, and hawks. There are camp robbers and quail. Wildflowers: paintbrush, Kinnikinic, Oregon grape, and tiny green huckleberries. We eat canned soup accompanied by the sound of flies buzzing lazy circles around the center of the cabin. Yellow jackets, grasshoppers, an occasional distant plane. Heat sinks down and the sunset glow begins to fade. Again silence—loud in its assertiveness. We call it a day.

Jeanne Yeasting
Bellingham, WA, USA
Hour 11

Yes, Please

A letter to Berthe Morisot

Dear Berthe,

Many thanks for the invitation. Yes, I'd love to visit you in Bougival. Not so much because I want to see your house, though I expect it's splendid! I can't imagine an artist obsessed with light and the ecstasy of color living anywhere dim and dull. No, I confess I want to lounge in your vast gardens—abundant, dappled bloom— roses, hydrangeas, hollyhocks. To devour all their tones and shades. To see the Seine flow slowly and calmly, day by day.

Want to kick off my shoes, like your daughter Julie, and wade in thick lawn; to spend hours in that lush enclosure. Want to see where you thrived in the Seine's river light. Enough to make the heart sing!

Victorian by birth you may have been, but you weren't invisibly demure like so many women. For that, I thank you. Expect me shortly.

Note:

Berthe Morisot lived and worked in Bougival, France, not far from Paris, at 4 rue de la Princesse, where she rented a house and spent every summer between 1881 and 1884, making at least 40 paintings: *The Fable* (1883), *The Quay at Bougival* (1883), *On the Veranda* (1884), *Garden at Bougival* (1884), *Eugène Manet and his daughter in the garden* (1883), *Roses trémières (Hollyhocks)* (1884), and more.

Vidya Shankar
Chennai, India
Hour 2

Our Mango Tree

blessing be ours for our second floor apartment
to be placed just where it is,
because, whenever we step into the balcony,
greeted we are by the foliage of a mango tree,
the most beautiful in the world

abundant is her outgrowth that the wide outer world
is obstructed from our view;
this evergreen is a world unto itself, and lost are we
in her embrace, as one would in a dense forest

wooden there hardly is anything about this tree,
her changing stability—inspirations for creativity,
her play of light—a photographer's delight,
as does her shade—a camera's crave on a fine sunny day

the freshness of her green foliage
mingling with the petrichor of a warm summer day
sends lyrical fantasies that go beyond the sensory,
while her leaves fluttering rhythm and romance
whisper metrical jingles into a poet's ears

often when the photographer and the poet
stand beside each other upon the balcony,
looking upon their common cause for enrapture,
they, too, become one with the crows and the parrots,
the squirrels and the sparrows,
the spider on that cobweb,
and the ants that traverse the branches—
creatures enveloped in nurturing love,
a gift of maternal care that the mango tree bestows
upon all who bask in her shade

Bette Low
Westport, MA, USA
Hour 2

Strawberry Shortcake

Summer fresh
Strawberry shortcake:
Tender, crumbling cake,
Spill of glistening berries,
Mounds of whipped cream.
Taste it!
Sublime, perfection.

Except, look close—
that berry holds half a worm.
You never know when you are eating a worm.
Life is like that, too.
It can still be sublime—
if you accept the worm.

Jill Halasz
Texas City, TX, USA
Hour 11

At the Coastline

Blue skies shine bright,
white wispy clouds smile—
a summer delight
if only awhile.

White wispy clouds smile
over specks of sandy shells
if only awhile,
playing in the turquoise swells.

Over specks of sandy shells,
dancing my cares away,
playing in the turquoise swells
at the coastline this summer day.

Dancing my cares away
until everything is alright,
at the coastline this summer day
blue skies shine bright.

Kristin Cleage
Atlanta, GA, USA
Hour 12

Floating

Rocked gently by the lake,
sun warm on my face.
Beneath, a silvery fish swims.
Cloudless blue above.
Children splash,
laughing.

Joanne McLain
Parker, CO, USA
Hour 5

Float in Stars

You float in stars
beneath stars,
poised on a still lake
composed all of one moment,
alone.
Would I be able to ride
that stillness with you,
hold stars within reach
yet not grasp them?
Can I be a steady light
for whatever the next
moment may hold
yet not yearn for
the light that answers
across the still lake of stars?

Rhea Kumar
San Francisco, CA, USA
Hour 7

Infinite

I stare up at the night sky dotted with stars,
and I am no longer in my body.
I float upward till I see what they are,
balls of fire, orange and gaudy.

I see Earth in all its blue and green,
a contrast to its unfriendly-looking neighbors.
Then I speed through the entirety of the galaxy,
past planets, moons with massive craters.

Now I'm in a galaxy far, far away.
I see a new planet from afar,
with sentient beings going about their day;
a planet not too different from ours.

But as I move closer, lo and behold!
There exists nothing but dust.
What I saw was a snapshot that was as old
as the light from it that I now touch.
I am back in my backyard,
staring up at the night sky.
When I departed, I felt tall, strong, and sharp.
I return but a humble fly.

Grace Wade Jones
Compton, CA, USA
Hour 10

Shadowed by the Moon

I am shadowed by the Moon.
When she beckons me to share her journey,
I follow her lead.

She has no eyes that she may see
and I try desperately to keep up,
but almost circumspectly,
she knows where I am.

Bouncing off mountains and skyscrapers,
as if she knows their height and breadth,
off every milepost that greets her in the sky.
The Moon has no tongue,
and she never lies.

The Moon staggers not at the glaciers
or the cold they impart.
Without legs, nothing impedes
her aerial performance.
She knows her way around
from start to finish.

Never pausing or looking back,
she does not leave me
and will not get off track.
The Moon shadows me.

Kim Sami
Campbelltown, Sydney, Australia
Hour 8

The Light Giver

In a deep, dark tunnel I found myself,
the proverbial canary in the mineshaft,
from a place of light above ground
that had become gradually greyer, darker,
and more menacing day by day.

There was a heavy, crushing weight on me
that pinned me to the ground,
pressing continuously on me,
making every breath a battle
of mind and heart and my badly bruised spirit.

It was a pit of despairing,
a cold, wet, lonely place,
where I thought no one could, or would
come looking for me,
let alone seek to rescue me.

A light shone, dimly at first,
from an unknown source,
just as I felt I could hold on no longer.
It seemed to come from the tunnel before me,
until the whole area where I was trapped was dazzling;
brightness sparkled off diamonds embedded in the surrounding rock.
I gasped with awe as the weight that had held me down so firmly
seemed to disappear into nothingness.

The light was the One who brought warmth
for my shaking, numbed body, mind, and heart,
infusing it with the joy of loving, of caring, of gentleness,
until I could rejoice in the awesomeness of life.

Elizabeth Wingert
Seaford, NY, USA
Hour 10

Illuminate

I can see it in the water,
Light that shines bright in mine eye.
Let it stay for the day
Until it sinks below the horizon;
May it flourish for now.
I can see it in the leaves,
Never to reach the other side,
Amazement as I stand in shade,
Thankful it shall be there
Every day of light.

David Hennessy
Glasgow, Scotland
Hour 12

Here Be Dragons

"Here be dragons" marks the places on the map,
showing the point where facts and knowledge ended,
and the wild places of the world beyond
where dangerous monsters dwell.

Obviously now we know that dragons no longer exist.
We drove them out with our reason and insatiable desire to know—
dragons survive on faith and mystery,
scepticism killed them.

Perhaps, together, we could find a way to bring them back.
But that would be impossible
because we already know that they do not exist;
we can't bring them back.

Perhaps one day we'll come to terms
with how we drove our dragons off the map
but we won't care about how this lost us
our imagination.

Is our world not big enough
to include the fact that dragons can't exist
with the necessity of having them—
the belief in something grander than ourselves.

Perhaps one day we will discover
a way for both dragon and reality
to live in the same world.
But then again, perhaps not.

The World That Is

Raven Kingsley
London, UK
Hour 7

The Season of Departures

The season of departures
was not predicted
nor announced
on lit up boards
or sheets of paper.

It came uncalled for,
uninvited, undesired;
and soon it was
so hard to breathe
through the ashes of memory.

Wendie Donabie
Bracebridge, Ontario, Canada
Hour 10

Mother Earth Cries

Humankind stomps across our planet
leaving destruction in its wake.
Forests decimated, species eradicated,
oceans and air polluted,
people starving, dying.
Mother Earth cries.

"When will you ever learn, when will you ever learn?"*

Want trumps need, grows into greed.
More factories, more roads, more buildings.
More money, more of this, more of that.
We get what we want only to want more.
We have no joy in this wanting, in these gains.
We compete to have the most,
without concern for those who have less.
Our human nature wars against our humanity.

"When will you ever learn, when will you ever learn?"

"It took a pandemic to show you the way.
It took a lockdown to open your eyes.
But will your minds, your hearts, and eyes cloud over again
once 'normal' days return?
Or, will you see how I, Mother Nature,
can teach you how to live,
how to heal the planet.
Together, we can heal what you have harmed."

 "When will you ever learn, when will you ever learn?"

* Inspired by the song *Where have all the flowers gone,* by Pete Seeger. I changed "we" in the refrain to "you."

147

Maritza M. Mejia
Miami, FL, USA
Hour 9

Quarantine

I feel strange,
lethargic in isolation.
Wearing our masks
is the new norm.
Zoom meetings,
working-from-home,
no social gatherings
or big parties.
This firefly-like sensation
as we pray for peace—
how much longer?

Sue Storts
Tulsa, OK, USA
Hour 4

Airing the Husband

My mother aired her laundry.
I air my husband.

He sits in the dark,
grumbles, gets
dank and musty.
Face transforms into
old bark and burls.
Lichen-covered, moss
begins to grow
on his north side.
He schleps up the stairs.
Watches the news,
yells at TV people.

He and the lawn mower
disappear to make noise,
cut things down.
He comes back
tired, dusty, surly.

I lead him out the door
into the light,
into the car.
Short trips to see sunsets,
parks, other distant people.
Warm breezes blow
away the mildewed mood.
Lines fade,
humor returns,
voice mellows.

For a while,
he smells like sunshine.

Caitlin Jans
Toronto, Ontario, Canada
Hour 8

The World That Is

In the world that was, I'd make breakfast quickly, only half
seeing the oatmeal slung into bowls. I'd stuff June's feet into
socks and shoes, check that her backpack contained mittens.

Every few minutes I'd check the time. There was always a planned trip
on the calendar, or a doctor's appointment, a play date, a haircut, the ballet—
all boxes I'd not even bothered crossing out come spring. Their cancellation
inevitable, Monday indistinguishable from Tuesday now.

Emily still wakes at six, June later, bumping down the stairs, hair
a tangle. They are never dressed before 8:30 and, in the early days
of lockdown, they never got dressed at all. Choosing nudity over PJ's.

We kept the curtains closed and shrugged. Our own work schedule
continued, snuck into evenings, time with the kids swapped between
us, a grateful thank you as we traded our duties. Touch felt loaded
back then, not just between us, but between everyone.

It doesn't spread magically, my husband says,
shaking his head. Over Zoom our friend tells us to treat
the virus like glitter. I remember years ago, telling
a carpenter friend about the pink glitter he had in his
eyebrows. He shrugged, said, *four-year-olds get it everywhere.*

I try not to think of that while I wash their hands,
scrub their hair, the world slowly opening up around us;
first the flowers, then invitations from friends for play dates.
We say no to the glitter, go on walks, allow the kids to shout
greetings to strangers on the other side of the street.

Jacob Jans
Toronto, Ontario, Canada
Hour 9

City Walk

I cross the street, afraid of a stranger's breath.
My daughter's hand gripped tightly in mine,
we weave through parked cars, a tangle
of strangers approaching from three sides.

My daughter's hand gripped tightly in mine,
we hold our breath, unable to avoid
strangers approaching from three sides.
Sunlight dappling the urban street,

we hold our breath, unable to avoid
the rigid set of rules we've chosen to follow.
Sunlight dappling the urban street,
I hand her a mask, ask her about

the rigid set of rules we've chosen to follow.
He should have stayed back, my daughter half-yells.
I hand her a mask, ask her
if we should love strangers, despite the danger.

He should have stayed back, my daughter half-yells.
We weave through a tangle of parked cars.
Should we love strangers, despite the danger?
I cross the street, afraid of a stranger's breath.

151

Marci Darlington
Mt. Sterling, OH, USA
Hour 6

Untitled

nothing scheduled...
endless possibilities or peace
doing zilch

Julianne Abend
Hewlett, New York, USA
Hour 12

not over yet

COVID-19 blur
wish I'd bought Zoom stock in March
still not over yet

Strength of My Loins

H.J (authorhj)
Canada
Hour 1

Influence

Moved by her eyes
and the way she never told lies,

struck by her fire
and her vehement desire for ease,

tousled hair, butterfly stare,
she had a gentle heart as warm as summer air.

She would grow to embody many things
while overcoming quiet tragedies,
creating tsunamis around the globe.

Unique, wholesome, and true,
she was a phoenix rising
shifting all that we thought we knew.

She embodied the best of life,
all the while making us better
with her sweet maternal flare.

Endless love
would she always share.

Solape Adeyemi
Ogun State, Nigeria
Hour 12

Strength of My Loins

I remember when you were first placed in my arms.
I couldn't get enough of you.
I never got tired of staring at you—
the perfumed smell of your talcum powder,
the oil liberally spread on your most shiny cape of hair.
I admired your beautiful pink toes. All ten of them!
I *oohhed* and *ahhed* over your exquisitely formed pink fingers,
the nails so tiny and rosy.
I kissed the soles of your feet over and over again.
I held you to my heart,
our hearts beating as one
in the sweet unison
of mother and child.
I was amazed that you had found your way into my life,
I was awed that you chose to grace my household
with your sweet presence. The love I felt, the love I still feel,
cannot adequately be expressed in words.
Nay, there are no words to convey the depth
of the love I have for you.
My heart beats for you, little one.
I try to peep into the future. I know one day
I'll have to let you go.
The very thought makes me shudder as I cannot bear it.
My mind comes back to the present,
the bundle sucking so tenderly at my breasts.
The nipples you hold between your
oh-so beautifully sculptured pink lips,
and your tenacity at ensuring all the milk
you can possibly drink, comes out!
I adjust you slightly when you're done suckling
to make sure you burp.
Your eyes look into mine, sated.
Sure and secure in the love, I radiate.
I love you so much, it hurts, little one.
I catch my breath sharply when your eyes meet mine.
I love you, my baby,
strength of my loins.
Together, no challenge is insurmountable,
no mountain too high to climb.
Your eyes close slowly after your meal.
I rock you, cooing softly.
All too soon, your eyes close in sleep,
your total shutdown in la-la land.

Kathleen J. Kidder
Hermitage, TN, USA
Hour 5

I Feel You

This biting wind comes too soon.
It feels brittle under this sandy canopy.
Though apart, we share
the same night skies.
Can you see what my eyes behold?
Are there stars shining to brighten you
with dreams of what is to come?
Or is your night too dark, too deep
with pain? Are you longing
for loved ones to come and lift
you from your couch?
I long to wrap you in love so sweet,
all else feels like a distant memory.
Do not despair.
Weep, if you must.
You are never far from my thoughts.
I am missing the beauty of your song,
your stories, your laughter.
Oh, precious one, remember how,
even at this distance, I feel you
in the uniqueness
of Love's heart. I sense it
when there is joy.
I feel it when your bones hurt.
I rejoice when your spirit is light.
Listen closely to hear
the God who loves us both.
Yes, the world has placed
cruel chains on all of us.
What comfort knowing freedom
those chains cannot hold.

Anjana Sen
Glasgow, Scotland
Hour 3

Homesick

'Are you homesick?' she asks, every time I call.
'No, I'm not,' I say, not homesick at all.
This, here, is my home since our baby was small,
her life measured in inches on my bright kitchen wall.
'There's really not much to miss,' I say,
apart from you, Ma, you live so far away.

'Are you homesick?' they ask, if I'm deep in thought.
'I'm not homesick,' I reply, truly I'm not.
This, here, is my home, this house we bought
in the land we love, where we've cast our lot
with the Lochs, the Ochs, the Bonnie Lasses,
the Glens, the Hens, the Irn Bru glasses.
The football matches with heaving masses
and Christmas presents with concert passes.

Am I homesick? I ask myself, when I'm alone with me,
winter evenings don't know what-o'clock to be.
I'm not sure, I whisper, but I do yearn to see
bougainvillaea bushes and a ripe mango tree.
Wall-to-wall sunshine ten months around
then smell the monsoon as it thunders down.

My two worlds may be oceans apart
but I'm never homesick, as I've said from the start.

Stefanie Hutcheson
Lenoir, NC, USA
Hour 4

Dear Ashley

To my...~~darling?~~

No. Scratch that.

Dearest? Unh unh. Try again.

Maybe you should just stick with "daughter"?

But it's so impersonal!

And?

Sigh. You're right. Let's try this again.

Dear Daughter:

Wait! Are you sure you should write "dear"? You know how she tears apart every word of yours—written or spoken.

Sigh.

Right again.

Daughter:

No! What did we just talk about being impersonal?

Well, then, what should I write? How should I address her? Where do I begin with this letter? Why does it have to be so hard?

I think we both know. Don't we?

Sigh. Right again.

Ooh! Maybe I should just send her one that's already written? You know, like a Hallmark Card?

Sure. And maybe you can start another battle because you—Miss Word Weaver—can't find your own words to say what you want to but must resort to using another's. Yeah, let's do that!

Fine.

Ugh.

Think, think, think.

I've got it! I'll send her an emoticon!

Will you never learn? If it's a smiling one, she'll think you are making fun of her for something. If you send one with compassion, she'll assume that you think she can't handle her life. No! Don't even think about sending one with hearts! I absolutely forbid that!

Well, then, how can I write to her and let her know...

Ahem. You must be dense! Stop typing right now. Don't even think of picking up that pencil. Drop it! You know better.

But I...I must say something!

Ooh, must you? Get over yourself. She stopped listening to anything you had to say years ago. And, no, don't even try reminding me of the fact that, years ago, someone used to describe you as the most hopeful person in the world. Surely, by now, you have learned that this situation is hopeless.

Sigh.

Sigh. Can you sense my mockery, woman? You are a fool if you think your words can heal, help, or offer hope. Why don't you just go and fix yourself some lunch? You know food always helps.

Well, I *am* kind of hungry.

Yeah. Of course you are! That's right. Go load up a sandwich with extra cheese and extra meat. Grab a Mountain Dew to add to the calorie count. The chips are on the table where you left them last night. Oh, and don't forget to grab the Tootsie Rolls to bring back in here for the real writing you still have left to do.

Okay. You're right. Again.

But...maybe just one more try wouldn't hurt.

Right?

Dear Ashley...

Nancy Ann Smith
Amherst, OH, USA
Hour 4

Hey, Mom

Hey, Mom, here's the latest happy news!
Andre, your first great-grandchild, is getting married.
He was just 12 when you ran out of time with us.
The whole world has this COVID-19 to worry about
but I know what you want to hear:
the glories and the struggles of your dearest ones.

Your parish is struggling, as are most around the world.
You and Fr. Tom must be helping behind the scenes
since Fr. Ratar has been doing more than seems possible
for two parishes now. The priest shortage is showing.
The younger generation continues to take church—and God—for granted.
And now the older generation is quarantined at home with the COVID-19 virus.

Your home, back from the years of building our family, still remains with us.
Your grandson Joe and his kids live there. They recently gave it a fresh coat of paint—
light blue in the front room. It was the first paint experience for 21-year-old Joey and Amanda;
Lesi supervised, all paid for by big Joe's wallet, thickened by overtime.
New sweets outside, too; white siding, black trim, greenery under the front window.
Their biggest struggles are employment and money—remind you of the past?

Your sister Rose and Cousin Katie are still here; 90-year-old matriarchs of the family.
Your Godson Rob has his Mom living with him, and she asks everyone who calls
to take her home. Her boys aren't willing to let go. They know she wants to come *home*
to you, and Jesus, and all the rest.
Aunt Katie still drives to the store once a week; babysits a dog for a recovering friend
since she outlived all her beloved pets. She prays a lot, and the world needs it.

We kids of yours are all doing whatever we can—some great stuff, some rough stuff.
Claudia's been struggling, feeling unloved in the midst of those who love imperfectly.
John and Dan are doing OK. Bill's been in the hospital twice this year and it's only June.
He's fixing the world in ways that will make you proud, but it takes so much body and soul.
Jim is getting angry, this Covid-19 virus and world insecurity is hardest on him, I think.
Linci's marching to her own drum—at the front of the protest line—protecting, helping.

I miss you. I look forward to seeing you again someday.

Love,
Your firstborn and most fortunate daughter

Jo Eckler
Austin, TX, USA
Hour 2

A Recipe for Christmas Eve Dinner

1. One freak North Texas ice storm
2. One recently widowed father
3. One recently bereaved child
4. Two frost-dusted Lean Cuisine chicken entrees from before it happened

To prepare:

Puncture plastic film and both hearts. Heat until unbearable. Turn on forgettable holiday movie. Sprinkle with silent tears and nods of acknowledgment.

Firefly Nights

John S Green
Bellingham, WA, USA
Hour 5

Summer Love

(a haiku sequence)

morning mountain fog
brush strokes widen
our appetite

overnight rain
sidestepping slugs
around the lake trail

autumn nap
the murmur of tree limbs
in silence

skinny dipping
under a galaxy
the flash of fireflies

I lose
a marshmallow to the embers
summer love

Ofuma Agali
Lagos, Nigeria
Hour 12

Eye Contact

Eye contact becomes virtually impossible
yet my breath speaks aloud from where I sit.
Easels of my sketches are filled with your alluring outline.

Congenial company is all I want,
on roads paved with sweets scents and deep sighs.
Nothing else will matter, so let your amity circuit light up my senses.

Tons of obstacles will end up amplifying my breath
as my eyes scuffle, itching to speak my desire
caught now behind your bars

to remain, until the floor releases your face,
until your eyes meet mine.

Vidhi Ashar
Bangalore, India
Hour 4

Special Chords

The audience has dispersed.
The claps have ended.
The spotlight is still on him.
As I close the door of this chamber,
all that remains is dust, his silhouette, and I.
After each show, he remains in that same spot,
continuing to play the piano. I wonder why he stays back.
Does the spotlight cast a musical spell on him?
My curiosity is not as enormous as my acceptance.

I observe *this* set of chords.
The chords that he plays during the show are swift and smooth.
They seem like runners in a marathon
or the shuffle of dance partners about to change pairs.
Right now, he plays mellow notes.
The kind that feels like an old couple singing songs from their time.
These chords feel like white silk draped over me. Time stills.
To share the silence with him is my acceptance of him.
His smile answers many of my questions.
Maybe it is I who casts a spell on him.
Perhaps I am the one he stays back for.
These special chords are solely for me.
And only this chamber, dust, and his silhouette shall know.

Anwar Suleman
Johannesburg, South Africa
Hour 7

Under the Starry Night

As the sun sets and gives way to the shimmering stars,
and the water laps gently on the bow of the boat,
I search for and entwine my fingers in your warm, soft hands.
As the night sets in,
a sliver of the luminescent moon
reflects off the still water and kisses your cheek.

Breathtakingly beautiful you are in this glow.
My heart constricts in this moment,
out of love for you.
I reach out to bring you closer to me,
to embrace you.

The boat rocks gently as our lips meet,
your fragrance permeating the still air.
All else melts away, just you and I
under the starry, moonlit night.

Felicia Clemmons
St. Louis, MO, USA
Hour 6

Perfect

Toes in the sand,
waves crashing into the sea,
warm sun,
slight breeze,
children playing, splashing,
a strawberry basil popsicle
cold and sweet,
falling asleep in your arms—
warm and safe.

Angela Theresa Egic
Astoria, NY, USA
Hour 11

The Castle

There's a place where
The land is green
As far as one can see.
High upon a hill,
He stands almost still.

Behind the handsome loving one,
Lit by the shining sun,
Is my castle true,
Red brick and lavender blue.
It's a storybook home,
Safe from any storm.

This place exists in my mind,
And the seasons are kind.
Existing in this heavenly place,
Greeted daily by his loving face.
There's only joy to behold,
Warmth when it's cold!
The winds cool our place
When summer is in place.

It's my place in this fantasy land,
With him and I
hand in hand.

Tanya LaForce
Muncie, IN, USA
Hour 1

Moon Love

in the shadowy night
she lingered
swaying nervously
bathed by the moonlight

in the dim room
he pondered
smiling incessantly
bathed by the moonlight

should they even question
these feelings
lingering passionately
under the same moon

she had been here with him
many times before
he had been here with her
many times before

bathed by the moonlight
she lingered, swaying nervously
he pondered, smiling incessantly
together under the same moon

Farzana Suleman
Johannesburg, South Africa
Hour 12

I Need You

like how a heart needs a beat
and a sentence needs words to be complete.
Like how a lock needs a key
and a ship needs the sea.

That is how I need you.
Without you, I don't know what I'd do.
You are like the peanut butter to my bread,
and the brains inside my head.

You know when I'm happy and when I'm sad.
Or when I'm disappointed and when I'm mad.
You are always there to wipe my tears
and cuddle me at night to take away my fears.

You walk alongside me during my toughest times,
you are my number one partner in crime.
You'll forever remain in my heart,
even when we are apart.

I just wanted you to know this.
Because this one is for you, Chris.

Nishant Jain
Cupertino, CA, USA
Hour 4

I Know

I wake up every morning next to you,
and with your eyes closed, I see you gently smile.
In that one instant, that one daily ritual, I know.

You understand me and I understand you.

I can have the worst day or the best.
I can laugh with you or cry.
I can share my dreams.

The day is only beginning.
And that gentle smile
tells me all I need to know.

With you by my side, I am never alone.

JC Sullivan
New York City, NY, USA
Hour 10

The Fun of Joy Riding Together

I'm being followed by a moon shadow,
moon shadow, moon shadow.
I may lose my eyes, my legs, my voice,
but I won't ever lose my imagination or my grace.

I close my eyes and see myself...
leaping and hopping on a moon shadow

above the fluffy clouds,
above the frenetic fray,
going just as high as I may.

Best of all, I'm not alone.
I'm with you, *mi amor*.

We're leaping and hopping on our moon shadow.

Shared joy. Shared fun. Shared adventure.

Never lose that. Never.

Naida Supnet
Pasig City, Philippines
Hour 9

I Long to Be on a Ship Right This Moment

I long to be on a ship right this very moment
and watch the men work in profound merriment.

As the anchor is secured, the seagulls visit
not minding the intense afternoon heat.

As the ship voyages into the vast horizon,
the world unfolds, clouds moving in unison.

Then the lights flicker as the ship moves farther,
and are replaced by the moonlight after.

Peaceful, serene, we will drink with the moon,
we'll pay tribute to Li Po and his love for the moon.

We'll invite love and the angels to sit among us
and enjoy the moment as the new day comes.

We'll talk through the night about poets and their poems,
or drift through songs by the ones we love most.

As the world sleeps, we can disagree
and talk of the books of Haruki Murakami.

I long to be on a ship right this moment,
because, husband, it is you I long to be with.

If only this were true, what else can I say,
I am happier, oh happiest, my heart's-a-sashay.

Krisha Anonuevo
Weslaco, TX, USA
Hour 5

October

As night settles into the cooling of autumn,
the lake mirrors the illimitable sky,
and on the dock, between the mirrored indigo in all directions,
we drift in the ether.

There is no sound but the drum of our hearts,
caught breaths of words far too afraid to whisper,
and the buzzing of phones that we fiddle with—
while I wait, you wait, the moon follows our hesitance.

Leaning in as the night continues to dim,
the blanket of your sweet voice offers the dreamy relief
of what I already know—and accept—
infused in the tears that fall onto your lap.

There is no need for somber sighs
to seek answers, to find tangibles,
when we can just continue floating blissfully
in the blue, hand in hand till dawn.

Nancy Pagh
Bellingham, WA, USA
Hour 4

Rold Skov

Some disappearance is literal; some disappearance is myth.
He forged portraits of Dutch merchants
when commissioned landscapes dried up. I missed
the witch hazel and bitter green willow gleaming
beside our bed. Old men's faces, slick as slate,
were something to drape my coat on.

Language makes us cruel. After the marriage he inked
my name in livid curls like a tongue of nettle
along his arm. Nothing that lives is nothing.
Months from now, in October, on a day of air
and yellow, I will find our tree in Rold Skov
to scrape our paired initials from its limb.

Mary Eugene Flores
Quezon City, Manila, Philippines
Hour 7

Season of You

Once we met, during an old summer ride,
just two young sober minds.
Banana cue with a halo-halo treat,
we walked home as we spoke.

Your dream was to become soldier;
an old, lonely profession.
You said, "One day I'll fight for freedom,"
but it seems like freedom killed your mom.

Summer's long gone, just as you are.
I wonder if you read those emails I sent you.
You're in a lone place with a crowd misplaced.
You left me through the rain of disgrace.

The rain sounds hard, blocking your words,
the last time you spoke with concrete words.
A scary sound was heard like a blast.
Months and months later, you were delivered as ash.

Kathryn Trudeau
Valparaiso, IN, USA
Hour 9

Firefly Nights

Watching them glow in the dusk,
bottle up the moment—
it's your last summer here.

Masking our fear of the future,
we listen to the bugs zoom
in the steamy night air.

The heat of the day fades
as the moonlight hits the tree-line.
I still think of you

on those warm summer nights
when the fireflies come out
and the moon keeps watch.

Leroy Leonard
Centennial, CO, US
Hour 4

The Car

I'm doing well,
I hope you are.
Do you remember,
in the car

that boiling day,
the herds of pronghorn
we sped past?
Your shirt was torn

and I could smell
the desert heat,
feel the floor mat

with my feet.

I was afraid to speak,
could only stare.
The wind revealed
your shoulder. So there

you have it,
nothing more.
You probably guessed
I sold that car.

Alena Casey
Hawaii, USA
Hour 10

Break

waves break
waves break, break
hearts break, break, break
foamy waves break, take
seashell hearts broken,
drowned by spoken
salt words. Break,
break, break,
break

Qundeel Aymen
Lahore, Pakistan
Hour 7

Season of Serenity

my heart has been lodged
in a very colourful, pleasant domain
where love is an activity to play
with or without mindfulness
i have been deserted by a facial charm
but could not control the will and harm
that time was a time of helplessness
what an unmuted recklessness
and the fraction of time ceases forever
i vow to do this never
that fragment puts me in serenity
i start to enjoy the universe in cecity

Jilo Tisdale
Atlanta, GA, USA
Hour 12

Infinity

I would know you—
in darkness…
through space
& across time.
Yours,
always.

The Last Road

Ciudad Victoria Infancy

When I was younger than my brain can remember,
I was embraced by walnut trees, they became my ceiling;
my breath felt like oil from all those nuts falling,
my head choked with the creeping and echoing sound of skull.
There were no squirrels.
My blood tasted the same as that tree before me.
Someone in the background taught me not to be there, at the ground
where the bodies of revolutionaries and some witches were buried.
Abuelita said that her dad would visit some relatives near the aisle,
because nobody got flowers to the cemetery away from town.

Ciudad Victoria keeps all that rumbling in my soul,
remembering how the sound of locked lions was heard from the farthest place.
Turn off some of my biggest fears, but they are the ones that serve as seeds—
when time passes, my memory needs to buy this place
and save it in these words.

Happiness is fake if you standardize it.

Diana Kristine
Dallas, TX, USA
Hour 12

The Crossroads

I stand at a crossroads,
unsure and confused.

One way leads to something known,
the other into the unknown.

One way is easy,
the other, terrifying.

One way will please others,
the other is just for me.

One way I dread,
the other ignites a fire within.

One way is expected,
the other is cautioned against.

I stand at a crossroads,
unsure and confused.

Britton Gildersleeve
Blacksburg, VA, USA
Hour 12

Piecemeal

So many of my friends   even my family
want labels. Want each part of me divided
parsed into neatly organised
boxes   drawers   shelves   folders   trashcans.

My hands go into that grey box
marked in black letters   *worker*.
My ears should go into a piano bench
tagged with a sticky note   *where everything is music*.

My feet quiescent in an old shoebox
that bears the sticker *runner*. So many miles.
Nearby a roll of foamcore holds a collage
of ravens and foxes and nautilus shells. *Yūgen*
haunter of woods, who has no words for green love.

Into this basket woven by Rwandan women
I squish my ovaries identified as *breeder*
—not to be confused with *mother*—safely stored
between the foxed pages of a thesaurus.

On an adjacent shelf, beside a scarlet chop

my tattered heart nestles in a bird nest
barely large enough to hold its unnamed pieces.
Its wings are splinted now.

An arm is wrapped in a threadbare infant quilt
a cracked knee beneath a bronze tray ~
inside a lacquered box is a teacup stained
with tea leaves that knew the future once.

Somewhere among these scraps and shards
a compass might point north, and pieces
heed a lodestone's call. But perhaps words
are not music, and pieces never make a whole.

But possibly…music is the skeleton of language
and song lives within each name. I sing myself
gestalt of broken pottery, torn pages, lost ribbon.
I sing my own pieces.

Arundhathi Anil
Kerala, India
Hour 2

Silence

I thought a thought
and said it not.
My life's a maze of poems
and thoughts unspoken.
From silence to more silence
—not for the lack of thoughts
but for the love of silence—
an unconditional affinity
for the lack of noise
in a loud man's world.

goodbye, hello

crisscross cobbled streets, navigate stone bridges to find who you are.
don't be the person they want, walk your yellow brick road to freedom.

your past will chase you, so face your fears, make them creep along
sodden streets, seep into damp, dark recesses where they decay,
feeding the freedom you taste like sweetness on your tongue.

an end, a beginning, the door closing on a life 33 years long,
hear that groan as it closes tight.

say goodbye, say hello, like fireworks on new year's eve.
i know you're frightened but live the aliveness you feel.
that other life's gone now, dispatched to the ethers.

Anshu Sikchi
Chicago, IL, USA
Hour 11

Some Place

Take me somewhere
far away.

Someplace where no one comes,
where I am unseen
and alone.

Someplace incredible,
unimaginable.

Take me someplace
where the sun shines bright,
where the songbirds delight
and take flight.

Someplace magical
and mystical.

Take me somewhere,
come what may.

Some place where thunder is heard
and rainbows are curved
and my purpose is served.

Someplace full of colors
and hope.

Melissa McCarter
The Hudson Valley, NY, USA
Hour 9

Wild Horses

Listen, I was like this in a storm:
brave, unanchored, lost in the moors.
I rose to the steel of the sky and fell back again
through howling wind and fierce rain.
Not happy, but edge-of-the-knife alive.
Alone.

When in this age I'm careful to shelter,
tell me about the wild horses
that run unbroken along the sea
when the storm roars towards them,
manes salted and tangled,
finding refuge on the high hills among the oaks
where they master the gamble of danger and thrill.
Tell me how the storm brings them together,
and returns them tameless and free.

Lexanne Leonard
Centennial, CO, USA
Hour 5

Safe Keeping

Tell me...

If the sky was covered
in hued umbrellas
keeping me safe,
away from the rain,
could I ever
put on my big rubber boots

and dance

chancing a sprained ankle,
wet hair, a cold to put me in my grave?

Tell me, if in that perfect, safe life,
brimming with hued umbrellas
keeping me dry,
would daisies ever grow on my grave?

Halle Hund
Eden Prairie, MN, USA
Hour 10

The Garden of Secrets

I heard the tale of a girl who became disillusioned with her life.
Her mother says it was school,
her teachers say it was home,
her friends say it was something else entirely.
They say she found a garden filled with all the flowers in the world.
She told them the flowers were special,
that instead of water they needed secrets.
And secrets she gave them.

Each day after school she stayed for hours, talking to those flowers,
giving them every secret she knew.
In return, they listened and listened and listened,
and grew and grew and grew.
Until one day, she arrived empty-handed, all her secrets spilled.
The flowers shouted and sshouted and shouted.
They shouted every secret back at her in one deafening burst,
filling her head with every secret every girl had ever told them.

Now her mother and her teachers say she ran away from home.
But her friends—they say she became a flower that day in the garden,
waiting and listening for secrets.

The Last Road

the road to hell is paved with good intentions
and I am made of them
I want to share the purest parts of me
but even the sun casts shadows
I built my heart to be strong
yet I see cracks where my good wasn't enough
I chose to be soft as often as I could
still choice hurt more than I knew
the last road will be my mistakes
and show that not all good is equal

I Exist

Harvey Schwartz
Bellingham, WA, USA
Hour 11

Acirema

What if the Native People in this country
had boarded giant canoes that took them
all the way across the waters to Europe?

What if they came ashore on the rugged coast of Wales
and took the continent by storm…seen as seers from far away.

Countries all wanted visits from this gifted group,
in touch with nature in a way not known in that day.

Europeans realized faults in their expansionist attitudes,
learned to live off the land with little waste,
and discovered a kinship with trees, lakes, and seas.

Kings gave away luxurious lifestyles,
went on pilgrimages to find
their inner selves,
and ended up in bliss.

The tribes flourished all over the continent
and wanted to share a more personal vision.

They took some explorers home
on humongous canoes.

What do you think happened
once they got to the place
that would be known as Acirema?

Megan Dobson
Austin, TX, USA
Hour 11

an open letter to Theodor Geisel

Dear Dr. Geisel,

There seems to have been a misunderstanding.

We were told that we'd be going places.
Well, let me tell you a thing or two, sir—
we've got a real mess on our hands now and we simply cannot
keep it under our hats any longer.

My friend Cindy Lou, who lives over on
Mulberry Street, says it doesn't matter if we're
red or blue or old or new, that every heart
should have a chance to grow.

(My friend Sam, I am sad to say,
has gone a bit green over the whole affair, although perhaps
that's neither here nor there.)

Now, to be fair, if I ran this circus it would probably be even worse.
But I know some very smart people, and oh, the things they think!
They say that if enough of us care a whole awful lot,
we could make some real changes around here!
I must confess that, while I didn't hear who first
hatched the plan, I'm behind it 100%.

Perhaps we can sit down together sometime and discuss these matters further,
but for now, I must go.

Yours sincerely,
Marvin K. Mooney

Tracey Saloman
Westport, MA, USA
Hour 2

Ringing the Bell at Church

Sitting in silence as the bell rings.
Memories not my own.
Four minutes for Floyd.
Four minutes for 400 years of slavery
in America.

Its echo shakes loose tears for the suffering and oppression—
their story and the story of my own people.

The bell rings by the hands of all the ages,
by the growing brown hands of my sons,
the Jew and Friend,
Christian and Witch.

It hardly seems long enough
as muscles burn on the rope.
Over and over and over
the bell rings.

Listen
Listen
LISTEN

A message too often silenced
with the privilege to forget.

Paul Sarvasy
Bellingham, WA, USA
Hour 10

Moonshadow

Loss, loss and more loss
lurching toward the ultimate loss
as a dimness
slowly, doggedly
shading and blackening
one's own realm,
unlike Job's sorrows
reversed at last as an enigmatic gesture
of reprieve and redress,
but more akin to Celan's death fugue
with Frankl's last remaining
human freedom to guide us:
the freedom to choose one's attitude.

Davita Joie
Boston, MA, USA
Hour 9

Madness

Our world is burning, fires of our own making.
Our children will never forgive us.
Madness grips them all like rabid dogs.
Dogs return to their vomit, the source of their sickness.

Our children will never forgive us.
How will we answer them when they ask?
Dogs return to their vomit, the source of their sickness.
The match once struck, cannot be unlit.

How will we answer them when they ask?
Madness grips them all like rabid dogs.
The match once struck, cannot be unlit.
Our world is burning, fires of our own making.

Protect the Children

LEAVE them in awe of your determination and with a collection of remnants from your life story.
GIVE them a lesson on your resilience.
TEACH them to hold space for your presence.
LEAD them towards an openness that closes the door to perceptions.
HOLD them gently within the moments you share.
LEAVE them with a legacy to carry when you transition and the physical can no longer be there.
GIVE them a playbook to guide them towards self-sufficiency.
TEACH them the truth about their ancestry and the power running through their veins.
LEAVE them better than you found them, so rejection doesn't drive them insane.
HOLD them accountable when decisions result in unfavorable outcomes.
LEAVE them with tools to access their own consciousness.
GIVE them the knowledge you promised to your younger self.
TEACH them love is not conditional but transformative in each individual.
LEAD them to embrace forgiveness and grace for themselves and others.
HOLD them in highest regards through praise and encouragement.
LEAVE them with a toolbox to create their own financial freedom.
GIVE them peace as they discover their own uniqueness.
TEACH them the importance of self-love, self-care and self-preservation.
LEAD them beyond the classroom to seek truth and initiate change.
HOLD them in times of sorrow and pain.

Carolyn L. Robinson
Baltimore, MD, USA
Hour 12

Why Do They Hate Me?

I am still trying to figure out why they hate me so much.
I know my hair is bold and nappy and will never straighten out
without chemicals and heat,
but why do I need to go through with that?
It is thick and full and I have the privilege to style it however I want.

I know my lips are full, but they help me to speak
words of love in every poem I write.
I know my fingers are long but strong,
they help me to hold on to all the dreams when I snatch them
out of the clouds and serve them up on a plate for all humanity to see.

I know my body is not the model size
but it has borne three brown babies who have excelled
in school and in life;
I love all the places where they made me thick,
left me adequately full—
full enough to teach them compassion,
full enough to be soft-hearted when so much of the world
is bitter and irate.

I am trying to understand why they hate me so much.
Why the thought of me standing up for myself
or even taking a knee would threaten some mysterious thing
about who they are,
who they perceive themselves to be;
it is not up to them to decide
who they don't want me to be in this world.

I have been planted by the waters of life.
I am meant to live.
I am meant to grow despite the knife they stick in my back,
despite the knee they place on my neck.
I am meant to thrive,
I am meant to breathe.

I know my mind is brilliant and that my heart is pure.
I know that I can collect butterflies
when I send out the message of love.
I pray that their worms of hate will never swallow it up,

204

that my words will not return void to me,
that they have power every time they are read again.
I do not know why they hate me so much.
Perhaps it is because I am so beautiful within.

Tamara Belko
Rocky River, Ohio, USA
Hour 7

The Season of Discovery

i knew this day
would come
& now you say
what i've always known
& i am afraid

for you

afraid of weighted doors & heavy judgement
of squelched opportunities

afraid you will hide from those too weak,
too blind to see your beauty, to see your kindness—
the one who always comes to the aid of others—

& now you say
what i've always known
& i am afraid

for you

afraid you will cower from happiness in a world
that seeks to define, to confine you to a box,
to label you—what they do not understand—

so many assigned labels which separate & sort
so many machinations unraveling human connections

& now i say...

rage against
all these little
boxes...

crush them!

together we will stomp the boxes to pieces,
those delineations of symmetry
which cut deep into marrow

together we will burn hatred with love
& leave cardboard ashes of hope

206

Brittany Greene
Charleston, SC, USA
Hour 12

Peace

they want peace
they call it peace
as if peace is justice
with a fancy wig
and flashy jewelry

as if calm streets
and pretty murals
will bring them back

they call it peace
when they mean suppression
when they mean conformity
when they mean complacency

they call it peace
and they want us to call it peace
to protect their economy
to protect their supremacy
to protect themselves

they call it peace
and they've got
so many of us calling
it peace

no justice
no peace
no justice
no peace
no justice
no peace

so, we don't call it peace
we don't call it a riot
we won't go back to
'normal'
this is the uprising
hop on board
or step aside

Sheila Sondik
Bellingham, WA, USA
Hour 7

Season of No Traction

Yes, Yeats summed it up
and we didn't listen.
We seem never to listen.

You know: no convictions, the good
up against the passionate intensity
of the ignorant, etc.

How each hourly travesty is
quickly eclipsed by the next
so memory doesn't function

as we need it to. Where to begin
to reckon the awful toll greed
and heartlessness

have already accrued? Nothing
sticks. The thefts from the masses
to give to the few, the infants

in cages, the medical equipment
hoarded in a time of plague?
Time to screw our courage and

our memories to a sticking-place.
The murders. The mud slung so far
just runs down our walls.

Pay attention to one day.
Call out the outrageous
with true outrage. No

traction, no action, no
satisfaction. About-face.

Jade Walker
Chicago, IL, USA
Hour 8

I Exist

I exist
here in the city
where big shoulders
tower.
But sometimes I cower
at the sight of blue and red lights—
the color of freedom,
hypocrisy.

I exist

And sometimes my skin's
a challenge
to an authority,
their eyes watching me.

I exist

Yes I do,
I've got a better chance of dying
from a bullet than you.

I exist

And that's just it—
I'm here
and my spirit won't
quit.

I exist

"Do your worst,"
I whisper.
Those ideas get us killed.
Even keeping your head down
isn't a guarantee
I exist.

And sometimes
I wonder why we're
brown.

I exist

And that's OK,
I think, as long as I
stand out of the way.

Diane Carmony
La Quinta, CA, USA
Hour 12

Elijah

He was the most gentle of souls—
playing his violin for the kittens at the shelter
so they would not be lonely.

On that night, he was just walking home,
carrying an iced tea for his brother
and, yes, he was singing and dancing
in his own special way.

For this, the police were called.
For this, the police put him in a chokehold.
For this, the paramedics injected him with a sedative.
For this, Elijah was killed.

I was just going home
I'm just different
I'm an introvert
That's all

Today we are all Elijah.
We are all different.
We are all gentle souls.
In this time, right now,
that is a tremendous thing.

Rainie Zenith
Melbourne, Australia
Hour 9

i want fruition

i want fruition
potential's a dirty word
gimme gimme now

Mahima Giri
Houston, TX, USA
Hour 10

Kindness

(a Brevette)

kindness
c r a d l e s
mankind

Season of the Poets

Linda Hallstrom
Sioux Falls, South Dakota, USA
Hour 7

Season of the Poets

They came together on a summer day,
tumbling and rambling across the screen.

They followed prompts or ignored prompts,
rhymed or roamed free.

They meshed and melded,
caromed and caroused.

An odd moment, this Season of the Poets.
No commonality among them—not of time nor temperature,
nor interest nor age.

Still they came.

They came for the words and the emotions and the challenge.
On this day-long season, poets flourished.
They relished and resented each creative hour.

Hope, despair, memory, fantasy,
whimsy, humor, truth, and irony
marked the season.

The poets owned the season.
The season owned the poets.
Magical, frustrating, exhausting, exhilarating.

Poets celebrate this sacred season in silence,
exploring thoughts, seizing words,
decorating isolation with ideas.

And when the day is done
and the season is over,
they emerge with renewed energy,
ready to revisit
the Season of the Poets.

Leslie Ferguson
San Diego, CA, USA
Hour 6

Purple Purpose

Will my voice matter
is every writer's question,
like coping
with quicksand

not sound as it sputters
      & reverberates
into the throat
or scratches & mars
the page

but worry
      hovering
at the back of self-
importance. Choked by diffidence,

I'm supposed to
write

for myself
because I'm called to words
      like a moth to flame
         & if words ignite
           ink burns

cinders remain,
lining annals of history.

Will my combustion resonate
is every poet's plight
      ashen &
disintegrating
      like remnants

whispering
        in
           the
              wind.

Maria Riofrio
New York City, NY, USA
Hour 12

Last Stand

Here, in this last hour, I have no voice.
Before, I fought out my inadequacies
on this page,
thorough and gut-spilling incisions,
verses shot at my own heart.
But this feels different.

Mediocrity has come for me
after a protracted pursuit.
I always wrote to defend myself, thinking,
if I surgically unearthed my soul
and put it on display,
the mediocrity would surrender
and retreat.

Instead, it is entrenched,
having taken up positions along all my flanks
not to attack, but worse, to mute;
so my ammunition,
my mighty pen against this sword
cowers.

And the drums beat in my ear:

No one can stop you from being an unknown writer.

Nykki Norlander
Sanborn, MN, USA
Hour 3

Voice

My husband and I are new to a small town. People are talking.
I watch the world pass me by through the window.
I'm afraid to walk alone yet I can't stay inside forever.
I would rather hide. I decide to try to wave.
I lift my hand and drop it before anyone notices.
How am I going to fit in when I am too scared to go out?

They say my voice is like a child's and that I'm as quiet
as a church mouse.

I am sitting on the front porch
in a chair that is like a hug. My cats are sprawled out nearby.
I struggle to wave as a neighbor passes in a red truck.
Being vulnerable is my least favorite thing.
Across the street, the cat hater is mowing her lawn.
I have seen her scare the gray cat away. I read books to pass the time,
peering over the top to watch. I'm too far away to eavesdrop.
Unlike my husband, I am not the first one to talk.

They say my voice is like a child's and that I'm as quiet
as a church mouse.

I have my notebook in my lap. I might go for a walk later.
Birds and owls fill my ears. For the first time, I am relaxed.
The next door neighbor gave my husband cookies. He said she is a homebody like me.
I am writing poems inspired by prompts. I waved to two people today and I am feeling pumped.
In writing, my voice is clear and strong. I'd rather write than speak.
Here, is where you can hear me.

They say my voice is like a child's and that I'm as quiet
as a church mouse.

Ann WJ White
Woodbridge, VA, USA
Hour 2

Recipe for a Ripened Intellect

A stream of books,
stacked in piles to peruse.
Grate science fiction,
mix in forked dramas,
and sprinkle particle physics
discovered in 420 BC
for added flavor.
History, biographies,
romance, poetry,
twisted about, squeezed for juice.
Vary the pages lightly
with a sautéed imagination,
add a liberal glaze of humor
to your mental gymnastics.
This recipe
of life and shadows,
served with a healthy
dose of sofa cushions,
provides servings
—unlimited—
for a lifetime.

Thomas Shea
San Antonio, TX, USA
Hour 10

To the Books I Can't Remember

When people ask
for a favorite book,
I never think of you.

It's a nonsense question, anyway—
pick a favorite breath of air.

Far rarer that anyone asks for least favorites
and lets me rip into tracts by dead white guys,
or that magical realism featuring waterfowl...

But you're still there,
far from the top or the bottom.
The stories that fade and blend,
authors and titles forgotten.

Like the ones by Clancy
(or his ghostwriter legion),
or the many fantasy tomes
where the elves are even better.

Your ghosts remain with me,
fragments of plot or detail,
phrases or images unmoored
from their narrative homes.

Digested, like so many workaday meals,
and made part of me.
Enriching me with shades and flourishes
learned not from some great master
nor crowded college class,
but from a novel I can barely recall.

By someone with the courage to write it.

Christina M. Rau
Long Island, NY, USA
Hour 6

I'm Gone

Been listening to *One Fast Move or I'm Gone*,
the soundtrack to Kerouac's *Big Sur*,
and it's as if I've been listening for years—
never stopping, always looping,
and making the lyrics my life
even when I'm not sure of every
word and even when I can't
remember if I read *Big Sur*
and if I did read it, if I
understood it and I probably
didn't because I love him
the way any woman loves a man
who drinks and writes
and runs around on her
and his words mean everything
to my little heart even though I
never quite get them because
they exist always out of reach,
in fast type scrolled and pounded,
and I could never live a life
like that. And still, I listen
to the lilt and twang and
I hold hope that something
gives so I can finally go.

Cecilia Hae-Jin Lee
Los Angeles, CA, USA
Hour 4

Nevermore

The early morning fog
was like thin milk hanging over the cliffs
and the cold air
filled my lungs
like breathing
through a cloud.

I always liked the early morning
stillness,
like it was a gift
the world was giving
for the early birds.

But that morning,
the quiet was interrupted by
the sound of deep breathing behind me,
which awakened every muscle in my body
and made my skin tingle like it could hear.

Fight or flight?
Fight or flight?

I ran faster away from the sound
but saw the dark figure emerging from the fog;
a creature so large,
its breath filled my fear
with each breath.

Its beak looked large enough
to peck my eyes out,
and though it was bigger than any bird
I'd ever seen in my life,
we both stared at each other in relief.

"Nevermore, Mr. Poe," I said,
as I tipped my imaginary hat at him.

He just looked at me and laughed.

Evelyn Elaine Smith
Waco, TX, USA
Hour 12

Clarissa Dalloway Buying Flowers

"Mrs. Dalloway said she would buy the flowers herself…For there she was." — Woolf, Virginia. (1925). *Mrs. Dalloway*.

Before parties, Mrs. Dalloway would set off for Covent Garden where she might buy flowers, picking out tasteful selections of peonies, tea roses, and lilies herself from among market stalls. At Harrod's, she shopped for choice cuts of meat and fine wines that the Bloomsbury set might devour as guests like John Maynard Keyes and E.M. Forster in their diaries, no doubt, touchingly recalled. For, as she said, there she was, "musing among the vegetables," a London dowager of an uncertain age, reflecting in a stream of conscious thought ever depressive notions of Post-Great War English rage.

Kevin J. O'Conner
Bellingham, WA, USA
Hour 12

No Oppish were harmed in the construction of this poem

According to the laws of the universe,
the free radicals that govern my life,
and a few thousand quacks on the internet,
all I have to do is watch this short clip
and everything I want will come to me.

But if the relation between a word and its meaning
is arbitrary,
I could end up with a Ford Transit van
filled with scholars of linguistics
and their pet gnus.

Or, you know, a thousand gross
of Bazooka bubble gum or something.

So maybe I should be wishing
for something completely outrageous,
over the top, beyond the boundaries
of good taste, with caterpillar frosting
and ninja star syrup;

complete the definitive translation
of every *shamon!* in the recorded works
of Michael Jackson;

or attempt to say *the happy man*
buys his canned ham wholesale
in Oppish.

Aah.
I really shouldn't be surprised.
Bands and bonds are snapping all over the place.

But now that all that's done with,
this is kind of nice, isn't it?

Gena Williams
Lenoir, NC, USA
Hour 8

Illiterate

Alas! The modern world is such
that I don't fit in very much.
Technology's left me far behind;
I'm about to lose my mind!

French I speak,
Italian, too;
and the tongue they speak in Kathmandu.
(That's Nepal, y'all. Nepali, by golly.)

I converse in fluent Dutch,
although I admit, not very much.
And I have a smart Pomeranian
who barks in perfect, precise Romanian.

But there's a tongue I just can't learn;
it makes no sense to me, by durn.
I even speak obscure Balochi,
but I cannot understand Emoji.

Who thunk that up, anyway?

Silvester Phua
North Vancouver, BC, Canada
Hour 8

Emotional Emoji

"You said you liked to text," said she.
And smirked, "Do you ever emoji?"

I look at her with scorn.
Such poor wit, such corn!

"Emojis are fine enough," I proclaimed.
"But they are still so limited," I declaimed.

For there are never enough of them distinctly,
to capture all my thoughts succinctly.

Emily Vieweg
Fargo, ND, USA
Hour 11

The Walrus and The Carpenter

When I was young, I thought
The Carpenter was angry that
The Walrus had EATEN all the oysters.

What I did not realize, was
The Carpenter was angry that
The Walrus had eaten ALL the oysters.

Let It Go

Ingrid Exner
Burlington, Ontario, Canada
Hour 2

Recipe for Joy

Ingredients:

1. Humour
2. Smile
3. Child-like Glee
4. Humility
5. Sun

Method:

Measure out 3 cups of Humour and pour into a large mixing bowl (container of you.) Add a handful of Smiles. Fold in 1 cup of Child-like Glee. Mix well to form a dough. Sprinkle in 2 tablespoons of Humility. Add Sun to taste. Bake until golden and delicious!

Aditi Shukla
Lucknow, India
Hour 10

Solitude

In this busy world,
where everyone is rushing to meet deadlines,
to make both ends meet all the time,
I wonder if anyone yearns for some solitude?

I wonder,
if just for a minute,
people would stop worrying
about the traffic jam,
about missing the train,
about the promotion they didn't get,
or about not being able to go back home for the weekend.

I wonder,
if just for a minute,
do they yearn for solitude?
For freedom from all these anxious thoughts?
For a time out?
For a few seconds to catch their breaths?

Solitude holds different meanings for everyone.
For a hermit, solitude would be a forest or a cave,
away from human civilization.

For a reader,
solitude would be a library,
where she gets lost in the world of words.

For a chef,
solitude would be a kitchen,
where cooking dishes seems to calm her
faster than any other medicine.

For me,
solitude is a cup of coffee.
As the bittersweet flavor wakes my sleepy senses,
I would pick up a book,
revel in the fantasy world,
live the lives of different people,
and travel far and wide
without even leaving home.

Solitude
holds different meanings for everyone.
The question is: Where is your solitude?
Did you even try to stop and look for it?

Karen Call
Aurora, CO, USA
Hour 1

The School Teacher

The envelopes came mostly at Christmas
with fat, jolly Santas or Currier and Ives'
prints, reminiscent of the ranching community
where she'd taught them during their high school years.

She'd gather the envelopes as they arrived,
set them aside, and on a snowy afternoon
or early evening in mid-January,
make a pot of coffee and have a piece of fudge
(or maybe something left from the holidays),
sit at the dining room table, wear
her reading glasses, and open the envelopes.

The letters told of their successes and challenges,
frequently with clips from newspapers
called the *Weekly Herald* or
The EveryDay News, and sometimes included a picture.

She'd look at them, touch the face, maybe say,
he lost his hair or *she's as beautiful as her mother*
because she knew their families.

She'd reminisce about where they
sat during her classes,
bookkeeping, typing, shorthand
or business law, and remember how
they'd whispered, didn't pay attention,
and how she'd despaired
of this or that one's potential future success.
Now she nodded, as yes, Jim or Elena
had risen above the inability to focus and
perhaps a challenging youth to make something
of himself or herself as she knew each could.

There was always news of their growing families
with pictures of their children. She read these missives
slowly, refolded the letters, and put them back
into the envelopes.

When she was done, she rubber-banded

the envelopes and wrote a note to herself
on top. *Didn't hear from Martin this year*
or *Suzanne got a new job.* The batch,
marked also with the year, was stored
on the bottom bookshelf with others.

Aymen Zaheer
Lahore, Pakistan
Hour 7

Seasons of Life

everyone is born to follow an order
this order begins from birth until death

every season turns into a new border
where we have to act until the last breath

the season of childhood is the most precious of all
ah! But it has to meet autumn's fall

this fall is the promise of a new spring
young age is like a butterfly on the swing

finally, it dwells in the den of winter
that vanishes, our existence like a tinter

Lisa Allen Hyde
Northern California, USA
Hour 5

Ceci n'est pas une parapluie

Magritte whispers, "Those are not umbrellas."
He is right, of course.
Those are souls that have been liberated
from the confines of hallways and corners.

No longer tethered to a human hand,
up high they can see
much further than they did before.

Their bright colors and patterns continue to
shelter those below and brighten the mood
of passersby.

When the breeze blows,
you can almost hear them,
planning their final escape.

The wires break,
the souls take flight,
disappearing into celestial heights.

Sangita Kalarickal
Minnesota, USA
Hour 10

Beliefs

My Monstera Adansonii leaves
have large gaping holes
where light breaks through on the other side.
Leaves with windows, she said.
If you peer through them, you can see
the soul of the world outside.
Sometimes, you can see the world beyond.
That's why the leaves have slits, she said.
Then she lit camphor to drive spirits away.

Toshia Stelivan
Texas City, TX, USA
Hour 12

Let It Go

I saw this guy in trouble
and I wanted to know his name.
Was it Jeff?
Was it Bob?
Was it John?
I could see the pain in his eyes
and the worry on his face.
I wanted to take him in my arms
and give him a warm embrace.
I wanted to tell him it will be okay,
let's have a drink and talk the pain away.
Let it go!

Mandy Brown
Central Texas, USA
Hour 8

Emoji Wisdom

The Sages rolled their eyes
at me when I shared my plan
to canoe across an ocean of honey.

"Let her follow the stars that rock
her to sleep," Curiosity told them. "Now,
now, better that than searching for riches.

She'll learn soon enough how to love
that house cat, Change."

Melissa T. Longo
North Babylon, NY, USA
Hour 7

Season of Unwinding

Luring myself into a trap,
I start unwinding. How obtuse of me
to ignore those around me, hindering
what I need to let go of those
that conspire and acquire!

Shaffi Kaur
New York City, NY, USA
Hour 10

The Song of the Lagoon

Allow for her song to guide you
to the crystal lagoon,
the song that will tear your soul
or your sanctity.

You shall taste salty tears of resentment
when you see where she resides,
waiting for you to set her free.
You will see pain and betrayal swimming in her eyes.

Do not let the beauty of the lagoon enchant you,
for it is just an illusion to draw you in;
the waters will scald your throat
and pull you beneath to drown.

You must close your eyes
and let the song of the lagoon,
the song of her pain guide you
so you can capture the silver lady.

For with her song, you can cure
the curse of death
and bind yourself to this earth
forever.

Christina Sng
Singapore
Hour 12

Anaesthesia

I fought against sedation,
swam furiously upstream,

exerting every ounce
of strength to get away

from the waterfall,
but to no avail.

From the moment he told me
to count backwards from 10,

the true countdown
had already begun.

The ice hit my veins
too quickly.

It superseded my will
and put me to sleep.

There was no fade to black.
One minute I was awake,

the next, I was gone;
like I was never there.

It was the best sleep I ever had.

Amy Bostelman
Austin, TX, USA
Hour 8

Liberation

Liberation from libations
Sans ale suds
Sans uppers and downers
No more dry mouth
No more headache
No more insatiable need for "more"
This is granted
For those who choose sobriety
You're either in or out
Saved by God's Grace

Index of Poets